HOW TO MASTER CHORD CHANGES AND HARMONY

By Sergio R. Klein

This book is dedicated to all of us – the knowledge-thirsty musicians of the world.
It's dedicated to those who came before us and left us their legacy; to those who inspire us today
and fuel our curiosity. And finally, this book is dedicated to all of those who are still to come,
who are about to bloom or haven't even been born yet. I hope those of us living and working
in music today can leave you something that fuels your thirst for knowledge and
your sense of wonder. Keep passing the torch...

Produced by Sergio R. Klein

Art direction by Sergio R. Klein
Text edited by Frank Cifarelli
Music edited by Sergio R. Klein

Acknowledgments

Special thanks to all my most important and beloved teachers: Toly Ramirez, Rodrigo De la Prida, Ismael Cortez Aguilera, Vladimir Groppas, Fernando González, Ignacio Díaz Bayo, Miguel Pérez and Ciro Vega.

Special thanks to my friend Frank Cifarelli, who edited all the text in this book. His suggestions, questions, encouragement and enthusiasm were an immense help. This book wouldn't have turned out the way it did without you.

I also want to thank my mother. My first mentor and friend. You have always supported me and fought with me to achieve my dreams in music.

Finally, to my daughter Mia... you are my sun. Since you came into my life, everything I do, I do it for you. Including this book. I love you so much...

Introduction

I wish I had this book 20 years ago. Back then, when I started studying jazz and improvisation seriously, I had so many questions. I became obsessed with harmony pretty quickly. All the interactions, the "moods", how they make music pull in one direction and then another and how they change music's colour and transform how we listen to melodies.

So much to learn, so much information, so many different opinions on what to learn and how to practice it. What comes first and what should be left for later?

I soon found that musicians in general have been really busy creating new ways to use harmony in music, but not really developing a good, solid method to start practicing these things. You know, when you're eager to learn – just you, your instrument and your love of music.

I put all of my "practice knowledge" into this harmony practice guide. The fact is there are very precise and concrete ways to conquer the harmonic language on your instrument. As I like to say: "to put harmony in your ears and fingers, so you only think about music when you play".

This book contains ALL the information you need to get there. Every chord progression you need to know; every scale; as well as where to play it and why. How different harmonic structures relate to each other and to our repertoire and how to better start practicing it all.

This book is a guide; a compendium of solid, powerful practice routines - tested and recommended by many music masters in the past, but never put together in ONE place before now.

This is why I wish I had this book 20 years ago. Every transcription I did, every hour of practice I've done, every conversation I've had, every interview I've read or watched... everything lead to this book.

I removed every non-optimal practice idea I've encountered. I've combined the best ideas into even better ideas in order to get the best results. On top of it all, I put all the theory knowledge you need to fully understand what you are practicing, why and where you can go from there to develop your own musical language... all of this to make you self-reliant and self-motivated in your musical growth. You will be forever learning from others your entire life, but you are the one who must decide what to do with the things you learn.

I truly believe this book can be a rock-solid foundation on which you can start to build your musicianship, your language, your voice and most importantly, your art.

It is all up to you now.

Sergio R. Klein

How to Master Chord Changes and Harmony

List of contents:

7 - Cycles   87

8 - Rhythm Changes   105

9 - Turnarounds   112

10 - The I - VI - II - V - I progression   141

11 - The Blues   154

12 - Epilogue   169

How to use this book

This is a method book. I like to call it "straight forward". This doesn't mean that you should necessarily start at the beginning and burn throughout every chapter until the end, only to shelve it and never look at it again. By "straight forward" I mean that I built a method that concentrates solely on the techniques that have proven to be the most effective for learning and assimilating the western harmonic language into your mind and fingers. Sometimes I combined several of those techniques into an even more powerful and effective version.

The key to mastering chord changes and harmony on your instrument is discipline and critical thinking about what you are doing and what you can still accomplish with what you learn.

If you manage to play every example from this book, you are far from done with your work. These examples are just that: examples. They give you an idea of how to keep developing your skills. What these examples are, however, are the product of very careful and disciplined study, trial and error throughout many years of research, work and, most importantly, proven efficiency.

This is why it is of utmost importance that you follow these simple, yet crucial guidelines while studying this book.

First, the most important one:

- Start by practicing slow, REALLY slow. Give your body, brain and ears time to absorb the new information. Once you have it in your ears, a good trick is to practice 8 BPM faster than your maximum comfortable tempo. This way you stay concentrated throughout the activities and your brain starts to learn how to react to chord changes. You will progress a lot by practicing like this.

Start slow and define the fastest tempo at which you can play ten repetitions of a given exercise without making any mistakes. NO MISTAKES. Write it down. This will be your "Chord Changes Comfort Zone". Now set the metronome to 8 to 12 BPM faster than this comfortable tempo. Eventually this will become your new Comfort Zone. Repeat the process.

- Every example on this book is confined to a two-octave range, so they can be understood by players of as many instruments as possible. You, however, should develop on these concepts in order to adapt them to your own instrument's capabilities and limitations. For example: Guitar players should play these exercises in all positions of the neck, but also use the horizontal "single string" approach (Mick Goodrick calls this the "Science of the Unitar") and the "string groups" approach as well.

- Every chapter of this book adds new ideas on how to practice every other chapter. It is expected that you apply every practice concept you encounter in a particular unit to all other units in this book.

This one seems obvious, but many people decide to "leave it for later" or just completely ignore it:

- Practice everything in all 12 keys <u>right away</u>!
Don't say "I'll learn everything in the key of C first and then I'll start practicing in the other keys". That is not wise at all. Practicing in all 12 keys right from the beginning will make you play better in C anyway. Just do it. Trust me, you WILL notice a considerable increase in your progress and self confidence. I'll remind you to practice in all 12 keys... A LOT!!!

PRACTICE IN ALL 12 KEYS RIGHT FROM THE BEGINNING!!!

- Transpose every phrase or motive you learn into all <u>modes</u>. Start by learning the most useful: Ionian, Lydian, Mixolydian, II and V degree of harmonic minor and IV and V degrees from Melodic minor. It is absolutely worth mentioning that you should write your own phrases and motives. Start building your own musical language right from the beginning. That's the whole point of being a musician, isn't it? To make art through your own voice.

- In many sections of this book you'll find new concepts and definitions - in one word: Theory (putting names to sounds and musical practices you actually may already know by ear). If you suddenly find yourself scratching your head about a certain concept or definition, just go to the Theory section and learn all about it there. Everything is fairly well explained. I'm of the opinion that music theory should facilitate access to new musical ideas and sounds, not overwhelm the student. I put everything you need to fully understand this book in that section.

- I deliberately didn't include any audio backing tracks for these exercises. They could have made the book more "attractive", but also this would have defeated the purpose of the book: getting your hands dirty. Learn the examples and record your own backing tracks. For non-harmonic instruments, there are always backing tracks for free on the internet. Even better, go old school: actually MEET with a friend who can play the chords for you and record him/her doing so. You will probably end up jamming together, an that's the best music school ever.

Ok, this one is just a good word of advice in general:

It is true that discipline is the key for success. Consistent hard work designed to correct errors, set new goals and plan the path ahead after lots of self-analysis and honest self-criticism. This is vital, not only when learning about music, but probably in every other human activity, too. The thing is, we musicians can sometimes confuse discipline with over practicing. We sometimes measure our work in "hours" instead of "quality of the achievement".
I've been there. I even had to be hospitalized a few times, because I didn't even allow myself to take a short break to eat. My smell wasn't too appealing either...
If you get overwhelmed: stop. Relax. Take one day off – a day where you do NOTHING related to music. This will help your brain actually absorb the information you have been feeding it. In my case, I had a "gaming Saturday". After a very short time, I actually made more musical progress. My brain was ready and eager to learn new things, I didn't need to spend as much time as before on working on one subject, because I could concentrate faster and longer. Beware of over-practicing!

Finally:

- Everything in this book is obviously deeply intertwined. You don't have to practice all of its contents every day. When you finish a unit (in all 12 keys!!!), then go to the next one. Repeat the process. It doesn't matter how long it takes you to complete the book. It really doesn't. Important is that you really feel confident in your ability to play any given chapter with confidence, without any mistakes before attempting the next chapter. It doesn't have to be at a fast tempo either, that comes with time. Every new chapter complements the previous one by adding something new. By learning any given chapter you are actually also learning most of the next one, so cheer up, relax and have confidence in your own work. You'll get there faster (and in better shape) than you think.
Once you have finished learning every chapter, plan a 8 day routine where you practice one hour a day to at least maintain what you've learned. To develop on it I recommend you practice one chapter a day for at least 2 hours. This may vary of course, but this is what I mostly observe in my own students. You might be a genius, but remember: Pat Metheny is also a genius... and he still practices a lot.

Now let's have some fun together, shall we?

Theory

Scales and Modes

In music theory, a scale is a group or set of musical notes ordered by pitch. A scale usually spans an octave and each note or **degree** divides this octave. In other words, each note corresponds to a specific semitone from the twelve semitones (half-steps) which make up a full octave.
The number of notes and its position determine the intervallic configuration of a scale, or if you prefer, its pattern of whole steps and half steps.

We can transpose that intervallic configuration into any of the 12 keys.

The Major Scale's intervallic configuration, its "half-step and whole-step pattern,"
is: 1, 1, 1/2, 1, 1, 1, 1/2

"1" is a whole tone and "1/2" a semitone or "half-step"

In the key of C, the pattern looks lie this:

```
C    D    E    F    G    A    B    C
  1    1   1/2   1    1    1   1/2
```

Each note from a scale is called a "degree". This concept is very practical for numerous reasons.

One reason is that a specific note or pitch could represent different degrees, depending on which scale we are using.
For example: the pitch "C", can be the "first degree" of C major; the "fifth degree" of F major; the "fourth degree" of G major, the "first degree" of C melodic minor, the "seventh degree" of Db major, etc, etc... So as you can see, it is VITAL to know what specific degree and from what specific scale a note is acting as.

Another very practical result of this way of thinking about notes is that by representing them with numbers, memorizing the intervallic structure of any scale and determining "formulas" for those scales becomes really easy.

To do this, we use the major scale and its intervallic configuration as a "mold" to determine the formula of any other scale.

The major scale formula is:

1   2   3   4   5   6   7

This numerical pattern reflects the scales intervallic configuration, so we know that between every number we have a whole step, except between 3 and 4, and 7 and the next occurrence of the root, one octave up.

```
1   2   3   4   5   6   7   1
 T   T   st  T   T   T   st
```

(T = Tone/whole-step; st = semitone/half-step)

The Mixolydian Mode for example, has every note in common with the major scale, except for the 7. When we look at the major scale, 7 represents a Major 7th.

The Mixolydian Mode has a Minor 7th though. Its formula looks like this:

1   2   3   4   5   6   <u>b7</u>

As you can see, to determine the formula of a scale or mode, we just compare it to the major scale and then alter the note or notes that are different using a flat or a sharp symbol.

On a side note: The term "mode" is actually a really old name for "scale". In the 20th century musicians started to re-discover these "old" scales, making them modern again. Fact is: You can say Aeolian Mode or Aeolian Scale. If someone goes crazy about it, give them a music history book for Christmas. This book would be a much better gift though.

Let's do a formula with a sharpened degree now.

The Lydian Mode has every degree in common with the Major Scale, except for its 4th degree, which in the Lydian Mode is sharp (or augmented). Its formula looks like this:

1   2   3   <u>#4</u>   5   6   7

Using formulas makes memorizing scales really easy. Just memorize the degrees which are different from the major scale.

The formula for the Lydian Mode becomes "just" #4. In the same way, the formula for Mixolydian is b7, and for the Melodic Minor Scale b3.

Easy!

The main scales in western music, from which almost every mode we use has its origin, are:

The Major Scale: 1 2 3 4 5 6 7

The Harmonic Minor Scale: 1 2 <u>b3</u> 4 5 <u>b6</u> 7

And the Melodic Minor Scale: 1 2 <u>b3</u> 4 5 6 7

If we construct a scale, starting from each degree of any scale, we get the **relative modes** of that scale.

Let me explain. This is the C major scale:

Now let us start a scale starting from its sixth degree, the note A. This note will be the root of our new scale, so we call it "1".

A Aeolian

1   2   b3   4   5   b6   b7

To fully understand this, you need to go grab your instrument and play all the examples. Reading about these things is one thing, but reading *and playing while you read* gives you an immediate idea of how ideas on paper actually *sound*.

You'll notice here that the notes didn't change, but their relationship to the new root is completely different. It sounds like a whole different scale...and it is! This is the Aeolian Mode. We obtain it by playing the notes from a Major Scale starting from the 6th degree.

Its intervallic formula is : 1   2   b3   4   5   b6   b7

If you play a scale from the 6th degree of any major scale, you will get this formula.

We can start a scale from ANY degree from the Major Scale. The resulting scales are called "relative modes". These are scales which share the same notes, but have a different root and a different intervallic configuration or "formula".

There are also the "parallel modes". These are modes which share the same root.
For example: C major, C Aeolian, C Mixolydian, C Locrian, etc. are all parallel modes.

Any scale you can imagine with its root on F# is a parallel mode to any other scale you can imagine with its root on F#.

I'm feeling really generous and professional at the same time, so I'll write all relative modes from the major, the melodic minor and the harmonic minor scales.

As a bonus you will also get all parallel modes from C, so it is easier for you to memorize all those formulas.

This way you will not only learn the formulas, but also where they come from.

At the end of this chapter there is a list of the most important modes, the ones you should master first. These are the modes you will be using at all times. There is a lot to practice so it makes more sense to start with the ones you will be using the most.

You can't go wrong to learn the other modes, everything you learn in music adds to your overall musicianship and creativity.

Every mode has certainly its own appeal, but as I said, the list at the end of the chapter is VITAL to every serious musician.

C Major Relative Modes:

C Ionian

1   2   3   4   5   6   7

D Dorian

1   2   b3   4   5   6   b7

E Phrygian

1   b2   b3   4   5   b6   b7

F Lydian

1   2   3   #4   5   6   7

G Mixolydian

1   2   3   4   5   6   b7

A Aeolian

1   2   b3   4   5   b6   b7

B Locrian

1   b2   b3   4   b5   b6   b7

C Harmonic Minor Relative Modes:

C Harmonic Minor
1 2 b3 4 5 b6 7

D Locrian 6
1 b2 b3 4 b5 6 b7

Eb Ionian #5
1 2 3 4 #5 6 7

F Dorian #4
1 2 b3 #4 5 6 b7

G Phrygian Dominant
1 b2 3 4 5 b6 b7

Ab Lydian #2
1 #2 3 #4 5 6 7

B Ultralocrian
1 b2 b3 b4 (3) b5 b6 bb7 (6)

The first modes from the Harmonic Minor Scale you should learn and practice are the 5th mode (Phrygian Dominant Mode) and the 7th mode (Ultralocrian Mode).These are the ones you will be using the most. The 5th mode over III7 and VII7 chords (sometimes also on VI7 chords), and the 7th mode over #II°7 and #I°7 chords.

C Melodic Minor Relative Modes:

C Melodic Minor
1 2 b3 4 5 6 7

D Dorian b2
1 b2 b3 4 5 6 b7

Eb Lydian Augmented
1 2 3 #4 #5 6 7

F Lydian Dominant
1 2 3 #4 5 6 b7

G Mixolydian b6
1 2 3 4 5 b6 b7

A Locrian 2
1 2 b3 4 b5 b6 b7

B Superlocrian/ Altered Scale
1 b2 b3 (#9) b4 (3) b5 b6 (#5) b7

The **Lydian Dominant** Scale, is the scale we use on EVERY non-diatonic root dominant seven chord AND the IV7 chord.

We use it over IV7, bII7, #II7, #III7, bV7, #VI7 and bVII7.
If I were you, I would definitely start by learning that mode.

You could say also that we use this mode on every tritone substitution chord. That's why we, as a "rule", use Lydian Dominant on dominant chords which resolve a half-step down. Think about it...

Then I would practice the 5th mode: the **Mixolydian b6**. We use this one quite a lot, too. As soon as you see a VI7b13 chord, the Mixolydian b6 is the scale to go to. Usually this chord comes before a IIm7 or II7.

If we are playing in a minor key, this is usually the scale we would use over the V7. It anticipates the minor quality of the "I" chord we are going to resolve into really well.

An example would be G7(b13) resolving into Cm6. We would use G Mixolydian b6 over G7(b13).

Sometimes this chord is misspelled as 7#5, and yes, the b6 (b13) is the same note as the #5, but they have a different function. By saying that the chord is b6, we assume that the fifth is unaltered, thus it doesn't use the same scale as #5, were the 5th IS altered.

We can use this enharmonic relationship to our advantage in modern harmony, but for the time being we will concentrate our efforts on the mastery of conventional harmony first.
This is absolutely paramount to be able to master modern harmony afterwards, so work hard and be patient.

The 3rd mode, the **Lydian Augmented Mode**, has some importance in modern harmony, it isn't necessary to practice it when you are starting out, but keep it in mind for later. It has a very distinctive sound and you can get some really interesting uses out of it to spice up your solos. I had to point it out as important though, because it is...maybe just not quite yet.

The **Superlocrian Mode** is the one we use on altered chords (#5#9b5b9). It is also called the **Altered Scale**.

The altered chord or "Alt", has every tension altered, the 9th, 11th, 5th and 13th:
We write "alt" to abbreviate "#5♭9#9#11" or "5+5-9+9" or "aug7-9+9+11"; which are different ways to spell the same chord.

Some say that to play over an Alt chord you have to "play a Melodic Minor Scale a half step up from the root of the chord". Well...that is actually playing the 7th mode of Melodic Minor/Superlocrian mode. I'm mentioning this, because, trust me...you will hear it a lot.
I don't want to send you unprepared to face the Music Police out there, no sir.

On Minor Major Seventh chords (spelled mMaj7, or -Maj7), we use Melodic Minor or Harmonic Minor's first degree, but this chord appears very rarely. I still have to mention it though.

Parallel modes

Parallel modes, are ALL the modes which share the same root.

For example, C Ionian, C Dorian, C Superlocrian, C melodic minor, C Phrygian Dominant, etc. are all parallel modes.

Why is it nice to think about parallel modes?

Well, let's say you have to improvise through 80 bars of Cm7. This is what we call a "Chord Vamp" or just "Vamp". Now, you could use Aeolian or Dorian the whole time and it would sound "correct", but also REALLY boring.

This is when you start using parallel modes. For example, play a phrase using C Dorian, then repeat it but change the 13th to a b13, a note from a parallel mode, C Aeolian. Then come back to C Dorian and maybe add a little lick using the b9 from Phrygian, and so on...

Combining parallel AND relative modes in your playing makes for some really interesting sounds.

LEARN your modes, practice them, learn their intervallic configuration.

A good way to warm up (I do this on a daily basis) is to start with the root of your choosing and then play one mode going up and another parallel mode coming down; then another up and so on. Make sure that you accentuate their most important notes, like the #4 from the Lydian Mode or the 13th from the Dorian Mode.

You can do this by just making those notes values double as long as the other notes:

Another good way to warm up is to combine the mode with the arpeggio. For example, playing up the arpeggio and then playing down the mode:

Obviously, there are infinite ways to practice these scales, but as a five-minute warm up, these two ideas work really well.

I will list ALL modes first, so you have all of them and can review the material later, but at the end of the chapter I will give you the ones you should concentrate on first. These will be the ones we will be naming and using throughout the whole book.

Parallel Modes of C - Major Scale:

C Ionian

1 2 3 4 5 6 7

C Dorian

1 2 b3 4 5 6 b7

C Phrygian

1 b2 b3 4 5 b6 b7

C Lydian

1 2 3 #4 5 6 7

C Mixolydian

1 2 3 4 5 6 b7

C Aeolian

1 2 b3 4 5 b6 b7

C Locrian

1 b2 b3 4 b5 b6 b7

Parallel Modes of C - Harmonic Minor Scale:

C Harmonic Minor

1   2   b3   4   5   b6   7

C Locrian 6

1   b2   b3   4   b5   6   b7

C Ionian #5

1   2   3   4   #5   6   7

C Dorian #4

1   2   b3   #4   5   6   b7

C Phrygian Dominant

1   b2   3   4   5   b6   b7

C Lydian #2

1   #2   3   #4   5   6   7

C Ultralocrian

1   b2   b3   b4 (3)   b5   b6   bb7 (6)

Parallel Modes of C - Melodic Minor Scale:

C Melodic Minor
1   2   b3   4   5   6   7

C Dorian b2
1   b2   b3   4   5   6   b7

C Lydian Augmented
1   2   3   #4   #5   6   7

C Lydian Dominant
1   2   3   #4   5   6   b7

C Mixolydian b6
1   2   3   4   5   b6   b7

C Locrian 2
1   2   b3   4   b5   b6   b7

C Superlocrian/ Altered Scale
1   b2   b3 (#9)   b4 (3)   b5   b6 (#5)   b7

Important Modes - master these first

From the Major Scale:

-Major Scale (Ionian Mode) for IMaj7 chords.

-Dorian Mode, for IIm7 chords.

-Lydian Mode for IVMaj7 and also IMaj7 chords.

-Mixolydian Mode, for I7, II7 and V7 chords.

From the Harmonic Minor Scale:

-The 5th mode, the <u>Phrygian Dominant</u> mode, for III7 and VII7 chords.

-<u>Ultralocrian</u>, the 7th mode is the scale we use for #I°7 and #II°7 chords.

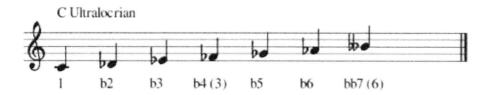

From the Melodic Minor Scale:

-5th mode of Melodic Minor, <u>Mixolydian b6</u>, for VI7 chords.

-4th mode of Melodic Minor, <u>Lydian Dominant</u> mode, for IV7, bII7, #II7, #III7, bV7, bVI7 and bVII7 chords.

-<u>Superlocrian</u>, the 7th mode from the Melodic Minor scale, is also known as the "<u>Altered Scale</u>". We use this mode mainly over the altered chord. An altered chord contains b9, #9, b5 and #5 scale degrees.

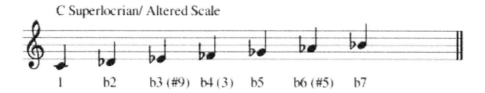

When you don't want to sound necessarily diatonic, this scale sounds terrific over any dominant chord. In fact, the dominant 7 chord can "endure" a lot. If phrased right, you can play all dominant scales on any dominant chord.

We will be working with these scales and their respective arpeggios throughout the whole book anyway, this book is about that after all: a practical guide to learn all this material in its musical context.

Just go through all the content, follow my advice and you'll be in good shape.

The "Right" Scale

The mother of all questions! Tons of text and explanations and confusion, but it is actually something really simple to understand and apply when learned.

Just follow these five general "rules" when approaching a new tune:

1- **Know the general Key of the song**.

Although in jazz, a song will rarely stay in the same key for long, it has a general key around which the whole tune revolves. Many of the modulations which happen in the tune will have some kind of relationship to the general key, and almost every time, the tune will finish on the I chord of the general key, so LEARN THAT FIRST.

2- on **I7**, **II7** and **V7** play the <u>Mixolydian</u> <u>Mode</u>.

    Formula: 1 2 3 4 5 6 b7
    Tensions: 9   13

3- On **III7** and **VII7**; play <u>5th mode of Harmonic Minor</u>.

    Formula: 1 b2 3 4 5 b6 b7
    Tensions: b9   b13

*sometimes it is necessary to adjust the scale for a note in the melody; in this case use 5th mode of Melodic Minor

4- on **VI7**, play <u>5th mode of Melodic Minor</u>.

Formula: 1 2 3 4 5 b6 b7
Tensions: 9   b13

5- on **IV7** and ALL DOMINANT CHORDS WITH NON-DIATONIC ROOT:
    bII7, **#II7**, **#III7**, **bV7**, **bVI7**, **#VI7** and **bVII7**, play the 4th mode of Melodic Minor, also known as Lydian Dominant.

    Formula: 1 2 3 #4 5 6 b7
    Tensions: 9 #11   13

Following these simple "rules" you will be able to play the "right" scale/notes on any chord in a "jazz repertoire"/diatonic context. You should learn how to do this as soon as possible. You must also be aware that improvisation is really an art form, and not just the skill of playing the "right notes" over chord changes. There are many scales and approaches you could choose to play over any given chord, specially dominant chords (those can take LOTS of punishment, trust me). There is "outside playing", chromatics, pentatonics, etc., but in any case, the four steps I just gave you could be considered the core of what you need to know to be able to improvise over chord changes.

Start by memorizing this information and practicing those scales with the exercises contained in this book. Once you start to master this, you will start to discover many new things you can try over your chord changes.
Anyhow, I will tell you which scales to practice on each exercise/progression at the beginning of each unit so you'll eventually start to hear all this information in your head. Your fingers will follow.

Modal Interchange and Transposition

At this point, it's necessary to add a little note about **modal interchange** and **transposition**.

The practice of temporarily "borrowing" chords/notes from another mode or tonality WITHOUT abandoning the original key is called **modal interchange**.

An example of modal interchange:

This is a phrase in **G Mixolydian. I**t starts on the root, then it descents passing throughout the b7, the 5th, the 11th and the 3rd, to finish on the root's lower octave.

Let's remember the Mixolydian formula: 1 2 3 4 5 6 b7.

Imagine that that G7 chord is NOT V7 of C, but in the tune we are playing it is actually bII7 in a IIm7 bII7 IMaj7 progression in the key of Gb: Abm7 - G7 - GbMaj7.

Ok, so we know that bII7 uses the Lydian Dominant Mode (4th degree of Melodic Minor) and that its formula is 1 2 3 #4 5 6 b7.

So what do we do if we need to turn that G7 Mixolydian lick into a G7 Lydian Dominant lick?

You guessed right. The only note which is different between those two modes is the #11 from the Lydian Dominant, so let's borrow it from that mode and use it on our original Lick:

Now the 11th is raised a half-step and we get the #11th we need in order to turn this Mixolydian phrase into a Lydian Dominant phrase.
This also changes the chord, because you are adding a tension which actually belongs to another parallel mode (different mode, same root), so now our G7 becomes G7#11 for its duration.

Cool, right?

Say we like that lick SO MUCH that we also want to use it over our minor chords. No problem. We use modal interchange again, but now instead of borrowing a chord/note from the Lydian Dominant Mode, we need to borrow from another parallel mode of G, in this case G Dorian.

Its formula should already be burned into your mind, but let's take a look at it again:

1 2 b3 4 5 6 b7

What happens to the Mixolydian phrase now?

You guessed right again. The only note which is different between Mixolydian and Dorian is the b3 from the Dorian Mode, so let's burrow that one now:

As you can see, the phrase didn't change, it is still a descending phrase starting from the root and descending through the 7th, 5th, 4th(11th) and 3rd of the mode until we reach the lower octave of the root we started with. The degrees of the scale we play stay the same. The only difference is that now we play the degrees from another parallel mode of G.

You can, of course, borrow chords/notes from any parallel mode as long as you stay in the key of the original phrase/song/progression.

So what happens if we keep the relationship between the intervals, but we change the key?

Transposition

Transposition is the practice of moving a phrase, section or an entire song into another key, but maintaining its tonal structure.

Let me explain with an example.

Let's transpose our G7 Lydian Dominant lick (fourth degree in the key of D Melodic Minor) to Db7 (fourth degree of Ab Melodic Minor). Remember: we want to play the exact same phrase – the relationship between the intervals in the phrase stays the same. We just shift it into another key.

Now the phrase and its intervals stay the same. The only thing that changed is the key in which the phrase is being played. In other words, the degrees AND relationship they have to each other stay the same; only the names of the notes, their pitch, have changed.

As you can see, transposition and modal interchange are VITAL in order to build and master your musical language. They are possibly one of the most important things a musician will EVER LEARN, as they let us adapt and transform our ideas to fit other musical contexts. More often than not, they inspire our ears and imagination to explore new avenues in our own compositions and improvisations.

A good musician should always learn how to adapt his or her improvisational and composition tools so they can be useful in as many musical contexts as possible. In fact, I will go as far as to say that this is one thing which separates the good musicians from the mediocre ones. That might sound brutal, but that doesn't make it less true.

Get into it!

Guide Tones

Guide Tones are the most important notes of a chord, and no, they are neither the root, nor the 5th. Guide Tones give a chord its particular quality. Put in other words: they determine if a chord is major, minor, dominant, etc.

Generally speaking, guide tones are the 3rd and 7th of a chord, and in some cases the 4th and 6th.

Yes, the root is also very important in a chord – vital, extremely important – but it is not a Guide Tone. The root can't tell us what quality the chord has.

CMaj7, C7, Cm7, CmMaj7, C7sus, C6, Cmin6; they all have the same root and 5th, BUT a different 3rd and 7th.

When the guide tones change, the whole sound and function of the chord changes. This is why they are so important for improvisers. If you target those notes in your phrases, job done my friend! You are outlining the harmony in your melodic lines. This may sound restrictive, but if you think about it a bit more, including these notes in your phrases lets you add some "less conventional" notes, some "outside" notes (there are no "wrong notes" nowadays, just "bad phrases" and "bad improvisers") and makes your phrases or licks sound more interesting. If you played at least one Guide Tone you are free, baby!

A simple practice tip:

When practicing the exercises in this book and playing your repertoire, try to target those guide tones. For example, always start a phrase on a new chord with the 3rd on the first play through. On the next, start with the 7th.

Secondary Dominants

Secondary dominants are **dominant chords with a diatonic root that resolve a fourth up** into all degrees of a scale that are not the tonic chord (IMaj7 or I-Maj7, depending if we are on a minor key or major).

A secondary dominant chord can also be substituted by its tritone substitution.

VI7 is the secondary dominant of **IIm7** and its tritone substitution is **#II7**.

VII7 is the secondary dominant of **IIIm7** and its tritone substitution is **IV7** (sometimes it appears as **#III7**, we use the same scale though: Lydian Dominant).

I7 is the secondary dominant of **IVMaj7** or **IVm7**, you know: major or harmonic minor, and its tritone substitution is **bV7**

II7 is the secondary dominant of **V7** and its tritone substitution is **bVI7**

III7 is the secondary dominant of **VI7** and its tritone substitution is **bVII7**

The VII has no secondary dominant chord, because it has a diminished fifth. In order for VII to have a dominant chord, the root of that chord would have to be non-diatonic.

Remember:

IV7, #II7, #III7, bV7, #VI7 and **bVII7** use **Lydian Dominant :**

$$1 \quad 2 \quad 3 \quad \#4 \quad 5 \quad 6 \quad b7$$

I7, II7 and **V7** use the **Mixolydian Mode:**

$$1 \quad 2 \quad 3 \quad 4 \quad 5 \quad 6 \quad b7$$

III7, VI7 and **VII7** use **5th Mode of Harmonic Minor (Phrygian Dominant):**

$$1 \quad b2 \quad 3 \quad 4 \quad 5 \quad b6 \quad b7$$

So, for all those chords, you just need to learn three modes when starting out. These are the "right" modes to play, the ones which express the harmony most obviously and the ones you MUST know.

Only when you master this knowledge (or are close to it) should you start to experiment with other scales and modes. I'm not saying DON'T do it, and I'm not saying you shouldn't be curious.

What I am saying is:
Don't let all the choices you have distract you. Focus on mastering these first so when you start experimenting with new things, it will be easier and you will already have a rock-solid base to build up from. Deal?

The Tritone Substitution

Tritone substitution is a term you have probably heard a lot when reading about jazz or pop harmony. It happens quite a bit, so I feel the urge to give you a short and good explanation of what it is and how and why it works..

I want to start by explaining what a tritone is, and why it is so important.

As you may already know, the tritone is one name we give to the interval that consists of two notes separated by three whole steps. "Tritonus", its original latin name, literally translates into "three tones" ("tone" is also referred to as "whole-step". A half-step is a "semitone").

Traditionally speaking, it is depicted as "the most dissonant interval" (that was ages ago, though. Now we are totally used to its sound). Even in the middle ages it was called "diabolus in musica" ("devil in music"). The reason behind this name was that, because it is the most dissonant sound, it was also the most distant from the perfection of God. Hence, it has to be the "devil's sound".

Well, this "dissonance" cries for resolution. In simple words this means we have to "release the tension" it generates – it needs to "resolve".

We find a tritone in the dominant chord, between its 3rd and 7th degrees. That is why dominant chords feel like they need to resolve.

Also remember that the 3rd and 7th of a chord are its guide tones.

Another really important feature of the tritone is that it splits the octave in half. A full octave is 12 half-steps, or 6 whole steps if you prefer.

C forms a tritone with F#. If you count the half steps between C and F# you get a tritone, right? Now count the half steps between that F# and the next C... also a tritone!

What this means is that the tritone has no inversion. Every other interval changes its sound when inverting it: a major 3rd becomes a minor 6th, a minor 7th becomes a major 2nd, the 5th becomes a 4th and so on. Not so with the tritone.

This is UNIQUE to the tritone and one key to understanding the tritone substitution.

Resolving a tritone in a dominant chord is really simple. We just have to move its notes by half-steps in opposite directions. We can resolve it by moving the 7th up a half-step and the 3rd down a half-step, or we can do the opposite and move the 7th down a half-step and the 3rd up a half-step.

Take a look at how this this tritone resolves:

This is G7 resolving to CMaj7 – the Dominant 7 chord from a major scale resolving to the tonic of the same key.
For the G7, the notes you should pay attention to are its 3rd (B) and its 7th (F).
These form a tritone that needs to resolve.

In this case, we resolve the tritone by moving the B a half-step up to C (the root of the tonic chord) and the F (the 7th of G7) a half-step down to E (the third of the tonic chord).

Now take a look at the next example:

This example is in the key of Gb Major.

We resolve this tritone by moving the F a half-step up to Gb, and the Cb a half-step down to Bb.

Now let's take a closer look at the Db7 chord.

Its tritone is, as in ANY Dominant 7 chord, the interval between its 3rd and 7th, right? In this case, these notes are F and Cb respectively. Now think about this: Cb is the exact same pitch as B. Hence, this is THE SAME Tritone (i.e. same notes) as in the G7 chord from the previous example. The only difference is that the B is now the minor 7th in this example and the F is the 3rd.

We have resolved the same tritone moving its notes in opposite directions a half-step up and a half-step down.

You may also have noticed that the Gb major key center (or F# major, if you prefer) is the distance of a tritone away from the key of C major.

We get a lot of very useful information out of this, so let's sum it all up:

- The tritone interval is a dissonant sound and we feel the need to resolve the tension it produces.

- ANY Tritone can resolve into **TWO different keys**.

-The **Guide Tones** of the Dominant 7 chord form a tritone. Two Dominant 7th chords a tritone apart share the same guide tones (the only difference is that their functions in each chord are inverted; the 3rd of one chord is the 7th of the other and vice versa)

- The 3rd of the dominant chord always resolves a half-step up into the root of the tonic chord and the 7th of the Dominant chord resolves a half-step down into the 7th of the tonic chord.

This is why we can replace or "substitute" the dominant chord of one key for another Dominant 7th chord whose root is a tritone away. We are resolving THE SAME tritone, just in the opposite direction.

The next example shows how the tritone substitution works by substituting G7 for Db7.
bII7 is the roman numeral symbol for the tritone substitution.

Here you can see another reason why the tritone substitution works so well.
Look at the root movement. It moves down one half-step. This is a very strong root motion and also VERY pleasant to our ears. This root motion is smoother than the original G to C root motion (up a fourth), and if you consider it in terms of a IIm7 bII7 IMaj7 progression, the root motion feels even smother (D-Db-C) and the resolution even more pleasant and "relaxed".

So now that you know what a tritone substitution is and how and why it works, it's time to learn about which scales we can play on that chord.

The tritone substitution for the **V7** chord is the **bII7** chord, in this case you know that over bII7 chords we play the Lydian Dominant Mode, the fourth mode of Melodic Minor.

The formula is, as you already should know: **1 2 3 #4 5 6 b7**, and it produces the tensions **9 #11** and **13**.

Following the 4ths Cycle

First Modulation Exercises
following the 4ths Cycle

One of the very first things you notice when you start to practice improvisation over jazz tunes or jazz-influenced music, is that the music doesn't stay on one key all the time. Going from one key center to another is what we musicians call "Modulation".

The purpose of modulation is to help give music a sense of direction, as well as structure. It also adds to the music's texture and overall movement.

Depending on the style, this can happen from just once, to many times in a single tune. Sometimes even a couple of times in a single bar...

Learning how to keep your melodic ideas coherent and at the same time changing keys is vital for a good improviser. The melody has to sound good and its notes must fit the chord over which they are being played.

Many students think that they should learn every scale and arpeggio on their instruments before even attempting to improvise on tunes. This is NOT TRUE.

The almighty John Coltrane once said: "no matter how little you know. Play what you can, but play it well"

Start by learning a couple of basic scale and arpeggio shapes on your instrument and start improvising over simple tunes right away. Learn then a couple more elements and improvise over some new tunes with a couple of new chords which use those new scales and arpeggios you learned.

Repeat the process.

This is what we are going to do right now: you will learn the four basic triads and tetrads, and then we will learn to modulate following the Fourths Cycle.

Why?

Because this is, _BY FAR_, the most common root movement in our entire repertoire.

Following the Cycle of Fourths Playing Major 7 Arpeggios

I want to start this book by showing you the basics of chord changes practice. It doesn't matter what level of knowledge you have, these very first exercises will continue to help you grow as a musician for a long time.

The easiest way to start doing this is by choosing a key centre and a chord quality, which can be minor, major, diminished, augmented, minor 7, etc., and transposing it into all other key centres.

The smartest thing to do is to chose a chord quality and a harmonic scheme you know you will be playing a lot.

Remember the Cycle of Fourths?

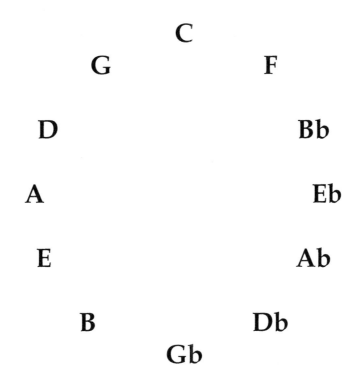

In our western repertoire you will find that a lot, and by "a lot" I mean **_A LOT_** of songs modulate at some point. This means that the key centre changes.

For example: a song starts in E major. Then at some point its key centre, E, changes to A for a while. This is what musicians call "modulation". Modulation can serve many purposes.
In the theory section of this book, you will find more knowledge about modulation, but for now I just need you to understand what it means.

Arguably the most common modulation you will find is the one which follows the cycle of fourths. Whenever the tune changes its key center, it moves to the next key in the cycle. Or, if you prefer: the next key center is a perfect fourth above the original.

For example: if a tune starts in F major, it would then modulate into the next key in the cycle of fourths, Bb major. From there, it could modulate into Eb major and so on.

The most common chords in jazz and pop music, ignoring all possible tensions, are the Major 7, Minor 7, Dominant 7 and Half-Diminished (a.k.a. Minor 7b5) chords. Therefore, to start practicing, one of the most practical things we can do is take one of those chord qualities, chose a key center, and play its arpeggio or any of its notes for, let's say, a full measure. In the next measure we do the same thing, but using the notes of the next chord in the cycle of fourths.

The "ultra-very-first" thing you should practice, even if it may seem a bit dull, is to play just one note per measure, and the "ultra-very-first" note you will chose to play, is the root of the chord, also known as the "fundamental".

Example 1

It may not seem like much, but this exercise is actually very good for ear training if you practice over a backing track.

You see, more often than not, when playing actual music, chords come at you in many different ways; inverted, their notes distributed among many different instruments (orchestration), etc. The bass player won't always be playing the root at the beginning of a measure, he/she may not even be playing single notes. Think about the bass on Michael Jackson's "Billie Jean". The bass is playing what we call an ostinato, a repeating melody, while the keyboardist plays the chord changes over it.

All these things make it harder for the untrained ear to identify the root of the chord.
In time, practicing this exercise against a backing track will help you learn how to identify the root of a chord very quickly.

You should, of course, apply the same exercise idea to any tune you want to learn. Identify the chords _by ear_ (you really don't want to use a Real Book or lead sheet when learning a song) and then proceed to play all these exercises in this chapter, over the tune you are learning.

This next exercise is similar to the previous one, but instead of playing the root of the chord, we will play its 3rd at the beginning of each measure.

Example 2

This exercise is very simple to execute, too, but really important. It teaches you to – guess what – find and play the third of the chord!!

But why is this important?

You might have already heard what a guide tone is. Guide tones are the most important notes of a chord – the 3rd and 7th.

The fifth is only important when altered and the root is important just for establishing the fundamental of the chord, but not its quality. The 3rd and 7th, though, determine the chord's quality. That's a really big deal in harmony as you can imagine.

We will talk more specifically about guide tones later in the book. For now, concentrate on playing these exercises perfectly until you get that "why-am-I-still-doing-this-boring-exercise" feeling.

Then do it for a couple more minutes. You see, this "feeling" tells you that you are actually internalizing the concept. That is your goal. Even professional football players have to warm up, right? Get the body prepared. These exercises accomplish exactly that: they condition your body, ears and brain for playing music. Touchdown!

The next exercise is a combination of the first two. We start each measure on the 3rd of the chord and then we play the root:

Example 3

The next one is a "proper" triad exercise. We play the chord's triad on each measure:

Example 4

Play this other one starting on the 3rd, then playing the root and 5th:

Example 5

Starting on the 3rd, then 5th and root:

Example 6

Some may argue that starting on the fifth is useless, but we have to remember that this is not only about harmony, it is mainly about <u>melody</u>. There are times while improvising where the fifth could sound more pleasing to your ears from a melodic point of view. And believe me, making good melodies is really important. There's a solo from Pat Metheny on "All The Things You Are" where, after a very long, beautiful and interesting phrase, he resolves his melody on an F ...over a CMaj7 chord. That is "supposed" to sound really ugly – it isn't called an avoid note for nothing. If you play F over CMaj7 out of context, it does sound pretty terrible. But in this context, as part of that <u>melody</u>, it sounds beautiful. It is the perfect note to end that phrase on.

That guy...

As your skills develop, you can start on any note you like (I love to start on the 9th or #11th for example). Remember, this is the "warm up". A very important warm up though.

Let's move on.

The next exercise is to play the whole tetrad (that means "four-note") arpeggio starting on the root:

Example 7

39

This one starts on the 3rd:

Example 8

The next thing to do to improve your arpeggio studies is to learn how to connect them.
We will use the "closest available tone" concept.

What this means is that after playing the last note of an arpeggio, instead of "jumping" to a predefined note from the next chord, you will look for the closest note available on the next arpeggio and start on that note.

Example 9

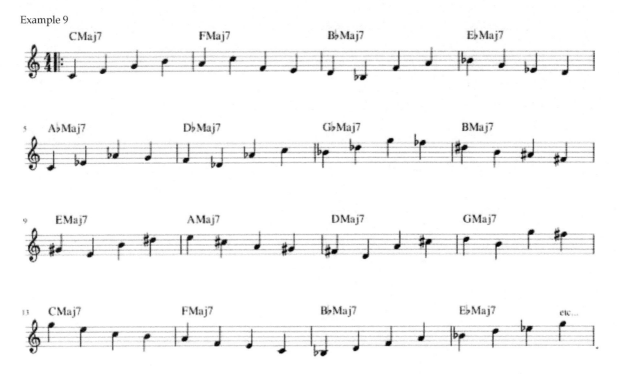

This exercise is very important. The ability to modulate smoothly between keys is really useful. You get accustomed to changing the key centre without breaking the melody; without having to jump unnecessarily to the 3rd or root. These obvious modulations are spotted right away by the "music police" at the back of the venue. You know... the ones crossing their arms, mostly average music students who haven't recorded anything yet, travel in pairs and like to talk into each other's ears.

Those guys...

... So, let's review what we have learned:

The ability to connect different chords and key centers smoothly so you don't have to "force" your melodies = <u>important.</u>

Music police = <u>unimportant.</u>

You get the idea.

All of these arpeggio practice concepts should be applied to each chord quality. It is not that I'm getting lazy and don't want to write each of these exercises again (there is a bit of that happening here, too), but I think, no, I ***know***, that using your head is way more beneficial than using paper the whole time. Think of which note you have to change so your major chord changes into a minor one, which is the b5 of Eb, etc. Doing this kind of practice is where the real learning starts to happen. Eventually you will "just know it", your fingers will go wherever you want them to go – you will have total control over what you play and when you play it.

I will give you some more exercises when we study the next chord: the Minor 7 chord.
Needless to say, you will also apply all of these Major 7 chord exercises to your Minor 7, Dominant 7 and Minor 7b5 chord practice routine.

Maj7 Chord - 4ths Cycle

Sergio R. Klein

Cycle of Fourths – Exercises Using the Minor 7 Chord

As the title says, I'm going to show you some more exercises following the cycle of fourths, but now we will use the Minor 7 chord.

The Minor 7 chord is really popular. You will find this guy everywhere. Mostly as a IIm7 and VIm7, but also as Im7 and IVm7. Two out of three chords in a minor Blues are Minor 7 chords. What I'm trying to tell you is that it is REALLY important that you study this chord so you can play it with confidence in any situation... and there will be a lot of situations where you will need this chord. Let's get into it!

In the Major 7 chord section, I've already showed you some concepts on how to start practicing arpeggios in a meaningful way – not just by playing arpeggios up and down, but instead using them in a musical context right from the beginning.

I want you to practice those ideas using the Minor 7 chord, too. Just lower the 3rd a half step when practicing the basic minor triad, and then lower the 7th a half step as well when practicing the tetrad:

Major 7 formula: 1   3   5   7

Minor 7 formula: 1   b3   5   b7

You probably already knew that, but hey, it only took seven seconds to write it down so, why not?

I assume that before you play the next example, you have already applied all the other exercises to this chord quality. If not, DO IT NOW! (seriously).

If you think you don't need to do it, you are WRONG, go do it!

On the next example, we are going to start each arpeggio on the 7th, one of the guide tones, remember? A very important note.

Example 1

Notice that on bars 5, 6 and 7, we have some notes which we could actually write differently.

On bar 5 for example, we have the note Cb. This is indeed the "official" b3 of Abm7, and when analyzing music, I prefer to notate it like this instead of B.

When writing music though, I prefer to write B instead of Cb. It is easier to read. It helps you save money in the studio: less confusion when reading notes = less takes = less recording time = less money.

This book is as much about practice as it is about understanding what you practice, so the notation I used to write that example is, in my opinion, the best to understand what is going on.

Here you have the notation I would use to make the lecture easier:

On bar 5 and 6, instead of Cb I wrote B. On bar 6 and 7, I wrote E instead of Fb. On bar 7, Fb is also written as E, and Bbb was replaced by A.

You may think this isn't important, but there are very interesting things you can do with enharmonic spellings (notes which sound the same, but are written differently).

Let me give you a small example before we go on with the exercises.

In C melodic minor, the seventh chord is Bm7(b5):

If we write and think of the Eb in this scale as D#, and use this note instead of D to build the VII chord, the Bm7(b5) becomes a B7(b5).

In fact, you could for example play D# instead of D on G7 (the V7 chord in this scale).
G7 would then become a G7#5.

This wouldn't be a case of playing "outside", because the note we are "altering" is in fact, a note which is diatonic to the scale.

I really love this fact of melodic minor; you can actually modify some of the chords without leaving the scale. It has more chords, than it "should" have. It's like one of those "transformers" toys which can transform into a helicopter AND a tank. Awesome! (I'm an 80's kid).

But let's not get ahead of ourselves now. I will tell you everything about enharmonic spellings and melodic minor chords further in the book.

To know that Bbb can be written as A, and B as Cb, etc. will be important for you to fully understand how harmony works and also how its rules can be bent for creative purposes.
For the purposes of this chapter, I will write the "official old-school" thirds for each chord.

Now let's get back to business...

The next example alternates the 3rd and 7th as starting notes on each measure:

Example 2

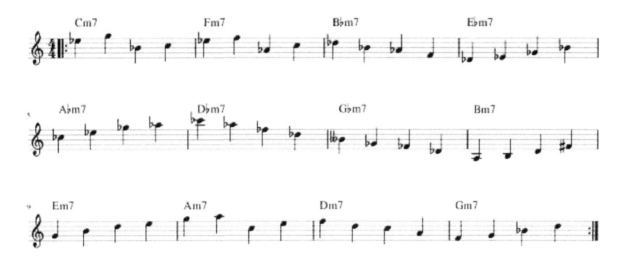

I am writing all these examples using only quarter-notes. This doesn't mean that this is the way you will play over chord changes, it is just a good way to start practicing.

You could take a backing track with two chords per measure. You could play these exercises without any problems over that backing track. The only thing you need to do is play 8th notes instead of quarter notes.

The same exercise, but now with two chords per measure:

Example 2.1

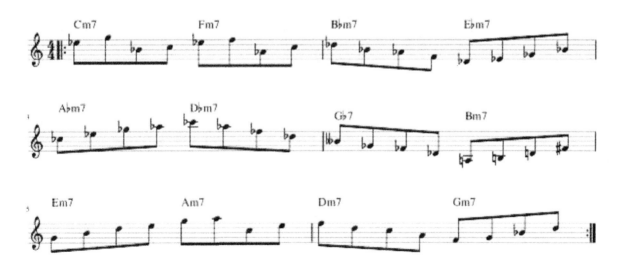

Most jazz standards and other popular songs are written this way. It makes a lot of sense, then, to practice all exercises in this way too.

On the next example I will combine some of what we have learned so far: connecting arpeggios at the closest available tone, starting on the root, 7th and 3rd.

I also want to show you something a bit different:

Example 3

Boom! A new time signature!

That's right. Not all popular music is written in 4/4... which is a good thing.
The <u>most common</u> time signatures are 4/4, 2/4, 3/4, 2/2, 6/4, 6/8, 9/8 and 12/8.

I know that music can be written in any time signature you can imagine – I and many others do it a lot. You can even find things like 4/4+3/8.
That's why I wrote "The <u>most common</u> time signatures..." and not "The only time signatures...".

And from those "most common" arguably the ones you need to practice the most are 4/4, 3/4, 6/8 9/8 and 12/8.

Why? Because the amount of songs written in those time signatures is ridiculously, overwhelmingly more than the songs written in other time signatures.

I know there are famous songs not written in those time signatures, like "Take Five" by Dave Brubeck, but generally speaking you'll only find very few of these examples among the hundreds of others in song books in any style.

Now guess which ones are we going to practice the most.

That's right! 78/7 + 1/13!!!

m7 Chord - 4ths Cycle

Sergio R. Klein

Cycle of Fourths – Exercises Using the Dominant 7 Chord

For this chord quality, I want to show you something new again. It has also to do with rhythm. I find it of utter importance to be able to play any rhythm you want to when improvising. Rhythm is one of the things which make your melodies and solos really special. It's of course necessary to be able to master playing over chord changes using 8ths and 16ths. But we also need to be able to play any rhythm independently of how "hard" the harmony is.

Freedom is what we are pursuing here.

But how do we train for this?

Let's start simple: Rhythm patterns

The first patterns we will use are the different rhythmic figures we get by dividing a quarter note into four 16th notes and then regrouping those four 16th notes.

First, we take a quarter note and divide it into four 16th notes:

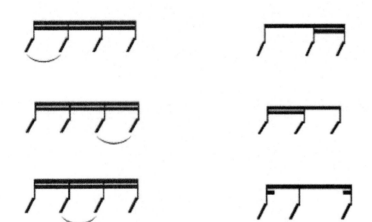

Then we will group two of those 16th notes together into an 8th note. We get three rhythmic patterns from this:

We get two more rhythmic patterns when we tie three 16th notes together:

These are all resulting rhythmic patterns:

Let's combine what we have done so far, with these rhythmic patterns.
For this exercise, we will ignore the first pattern of four 16th notes. In practice, this is the same as playing two beats of 8th notes and we have done that more than enough at this point.

We will use the second pattern on the list to create our first exercise. You'll notice right away that it is a three-note pattern, but unlike the 6/8 exercises we played in the m7(b5) chapter, the three notes from this rhythmic pattern aren't all of the same length. The first one is twice as long as each of the following notes.

The first exercise we could write then, is to take the ideas from our 6/8 exercises and apply them to a 4/4 measure.

The original idea from our m7(b5) exercises looks like this:

Now we will of course change the notes so we get a dominant chord, and we will also play two chords per measure. It is a bit more challenging, but if you've been working through all the exercises thus far, you will nail it in no time. Start slowly at first and then speed it up.

Exercise 1

You will notice how different this exercise feels from everything we have done so far. We are still playing a triad arpeggio over a tetrad chord, and we are also dividing each beat in multiples of three. The difference is that not all of the notes have the same length. Our brain has more time to think about the note that is coming next while playing some notes, and less time while playing other notes. This is something you *must* learn, to the point where you don't feel that some notes are more difficult than others while playing. In other words: you don't get distracted from the music.

Rhythm is something you must *never* ignore nor "leave for later". Start getting this into your fingers right now.

Let's try tetrads and another rhythmic pattern now:

Exercise 2

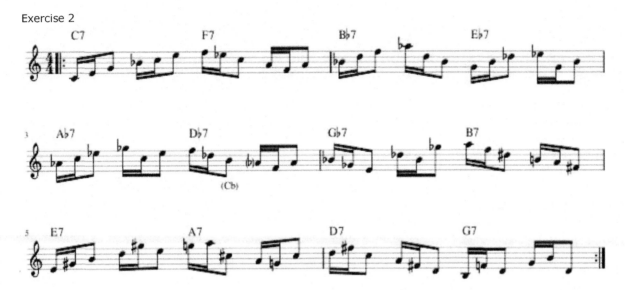

On this example I didn't choose the same degree of each chord to start each arpeggio. Instead I randomly started on the root, 3rd and 7th. In each case though, they were the closest tone available.

The next exercise features something I like to do a lot: combining rhythmic patterns. We will play a different rhythmic pattern on each *chord*.

Exercise 3

It's getting fun, right?

The next exercise is very similar, but now we change the pattern on each *beat*.

Exercise 4

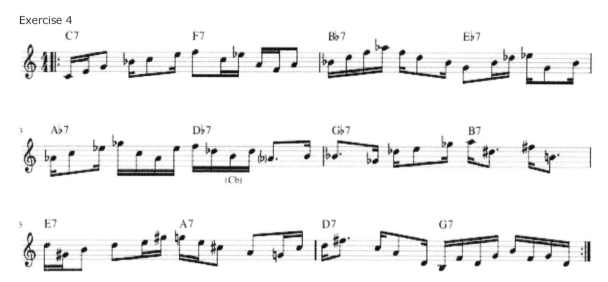

I really encourage you to apply these ideas to ALL the exercises in this book. In further chapters I'll show you many examples of the most important chord progressions and music forms you need to master when venturing into the world of chord changes.

I want you to apply these rhythmic concepts to all of those chord changes exercises. We've really only scratched the surface in this chapter. For example, in exercise one, I showed to you how to apply rhythmic patterns to your arpeggio practice using just one pattern. You need to do this using all rhythmic patterns I showed to you, plus others you may know.

Here is another example of what you can do. Let's add some triplets combined with the patterns we have been using so far.

Exercise 5

This example may seem exaggerated at first, but you only need to listen to rhythm masters like Herbie Hancock, Scott Henderson, Wayne Krantz or Michael Brecker (among others) for a second to realize that you really need to master your rhythmic capabilities. In college, I attended a masterclass by Herbie Hancock. Guess which topic he started with. That's right: rhythm!

He encouraged us to *really* practice rhythm, so that we never get distracted by any technique or rhythmic limitations we may have. This frees the mind and ears to make real music. In this way, you'll never have to alter the melodies in your head due to their complexity.

It is a very long process to really master rhythm like these musicians have, but all that is behind the marvelous music they make is hard work. Talent? Sure! But you've got that, too. You are seeking knowledge in this book, after all. All you need, all *we* need, is to work hard and find happiness in doing so. Music is a wonderful thing to do and to live for.

Ok let's go crazier now.

What if we get some more rhythmic patterns, but now out of the triplets?

That was a rhetorical question, of course. I have the graphic files ready, so here we go!

The first thing we are going to do is divide two of the three 8th notes into 16th notes:

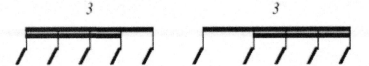

Pick just one note to begin with and repeat the figure until it feels comfortable under your fingers. After a couple of minutes switch to the second pattern and repeat the procedure.

Once you have nailed those two, we can move on.

You may have noticed (of COURSE you noticed!) that on both patterns we have a 16th note grouping. Yes, you guessed right! Now we will apply the 16th note patterns we have already learned in the 8th note exercises to the 16th notes in the triplet patterns.

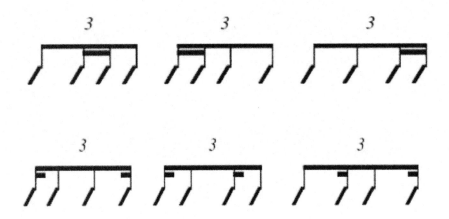

In preparation for the next big unit in this book, the study of the II V I Progression, we will practice over II V chord changes. These are of course the chords build off the second and fifth degrees of a scale respectively. Their functions, as you might already know, are subdominant (the II chord) and dominant (the V chord). Do not confuse harmonic function with degree. Different degrees could have the same harmonic function in music. For example, the 7th scale degree acts as a substitution of the 5th degree. Both have the same harmonic function of <u>dominant</u>. In the same manner, the II chord is called supertonic, when referred to as the second degree of a scale. Its *<u>harmonic function is subdominant,</u>* though. In the past the IV chord, the subdominant chord by definition, was used way more than nowadays. In the 20th century, we got accustomed to hearing the root motion of the II V progression which follows the cycle of fourths. It is a pleasant sound to us. One could say that the II V chord motion has been "abused"… because of that, we must master it. The II V in a II V I chord progression is present so often in music that it cannot be ignored by any musician interested in popular music style like jazz, blues, funk or any kind of pop. So here we are: I'm writing about it and you are reading about it.

Now it's time to practice it.

Dominant 7 Chord - 4ths Cycle

Sergio R. Klein

Cycle of Fourths – Exercises Using the Minor 7(b5) Chord

This chord quality – also known as "half diminished" – is extensively present in our music.
It's "half diminished" name comes from the fact that its 7th is minor (two half-steps down from the root) and not diminished (three half-steps down from the root) as in a fully diminished 7th chord.

It is most commonly used as IIm7(b5) in a minor II V I. Other uses are: The diatonic chord built off the 6th scale degree in melodic minor and as VIIm7(b5) substituting a V7 in a major key.

In the previous unit, I promised you some exercises in other time signatures and that's exactly what I'm going to show you here.

I think that 6/8 is more a "game changer" than 3/4. Each beat is divided in three equal notes. This type of time signature is classified as a kind of "compound meter".

3/4, 4/4, 6/4, 2/2 time signatures are called "simple", because each beat is divided in two equal notes.

Don't confuse this with "triple" or "quadruple" measures, they refer to the amount of beats per measure, not the number of notes per beat.

A 3/4 measure is classified as "simple triple meter". Each measure has three beats and each beat can be divided in multiples of two.

The 6/8 measure is classified as "compound duple meter". Each measure has two beats, and each of those beats can be divided in three equal notes.

Compound time signatures have dotted notes as their beat.

The difference in feel between compound and simple meters is very noticeable while playing and practicing.

The difference between a 6/8 measure and a 4/4 measure is more dramatic than between a 3/4 and a 4/4. There is a beat every three eighth notes. In a 3/4 measure there is a beat every two eighth notes. Even your body moves differently when listening to compound time signatures.

This definitely plays a role in how you internally hear the melodies you want to play. If you don't practice compound time signatures, It will become an issue to get your fingers to play what you are hearing.

Let's start with the exercises. Since we are big boys and girls now, I will write the double-flat notes as unaltered notes now. Bbb will be written as C and so forth.

Why?

Because it makes you think. Thinking is a good thing. It forces you to analyze what you are doing and compare it with other things you may know. This is one of the practices that inevitably will lead you to develop your own musical language.

You might not realize it right away, but if you keep thinking about and analyzing what you play, you will.

The first example is quite simple. Triads played up from the root:

Example 1

The next one is the same idea, but playing tetrads:

Example 2

Now Let's start on the 3rd:

Example 3

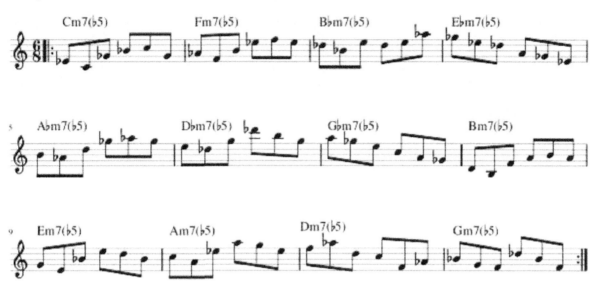

Although you don't have the same "pattern" on every measure, I made sure they all start the same and connect at the closest tone available.
If you get used to connecting different arpeggios using this very simple to understand concept, you can do practically anything while playing on one chord.

Here is an example of what I mean by this:

Example 3a

etc...

While the intervals played during a single chord are pretty wide in this example, the connection between each measure is still at the closest available tone. In this example I targeted the 3rd again at the beginning of each new chord. You can go crazier than this of course. I just wanted to show you how important it is to make a smooth connection between different chords while playing over chord changes.

This doesn't mean that when you are playing real music with your friends and esteemed colleges you must always play changes in this way. Sometimes your intuition will say "Jump now, man! That would be really cool and dramatic!". When your intuition tells you things like this you should use the force and go with it. What could possibly go wrong? Besides the empire, of course...

In all seriousness now: being able to connect arpeggios/harmonies smoothly is a really powerful tool to have at your disposal, especially when connecting harmonies from different key centers. You could summarize the concept like this:

Don't jump to connect chords because it is the only thing you can do. Only jump when your melody wants to jump.

m7(b5) Chord - 4ths Cycle

Sergio R. Klein

Warming up for the II V I Cadence

II V Exercises - Warming Up for II V I Studies

Since we have already practiced a lot using all basic chord qualities, you'll be able to ease right into this exercise.

We will start by playing a IIm7 V7 in the key of C major and then continue to play the same progression in every key following the cycle of fourths. It's a good exercise, because the I chord isn't present. This will help you learn to identify the key in which you are playing without having to hear the I chord. Besides that, you will encounter a lot of unresolved II V progressions in many tunes. Usually what follows is another II V or II V I a perfect fourth above the root of the first V chord, like this: Dm7 G7 Cm7 F7. I'll save that for the second exercise, though.

In this one, as I said, we will follow the cycle of fourths and use just one rhythmic pattern derived from the triplet:

Exercise 1

60

For the next exercise we will use another rhythmic pattern derived from the triplet:

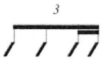

We're also going to use a different modulation. Instead of changing <u>keys</u> following the cycle of fourths, we will change the root of <u>*every chord*</u> following the cycle of fourths.

The result of the chords always following this root motion is that every II V progression modulates down a whole step from the previous one.
If the first measure is in the key of C, the second one will be in the key of Bb, and so on.

As I said, the root movement of each chord will follow the cycle of fourths.

The II V in the key of C is <u>**D**</u>m7 <u>**G**</u>7 and in the key of Bb is <u>**C**</u>m7 <u>**F**</u>7.

The roots D to G to C to F all follow the cycle of fourths. This pattern repeats throughout the exercise.

Exercise 2

If you find a new exercise too challenging, don't be too hard on yourself. Practice it in another way that's easier for you. You could, for example, play this last exercise without the rhythmic pattern when first learning it. Or just play triads. Apply a concept you have already mastered or just make yourself a slower backing track and practice using that.
There is no rush!

The important thing is that you don't give up when finding something too difficult at any given time. Just make it easier by changing the rhythm, practicing slower, etc. Do whatever you need to in order to start internalizing these exercises as music.

The most important thing is to NEVER stop practicing. *Take it easy*. Enjoy the ride.

The II V I Cadence

The "II - V - I" Progression

Well my friend, if you want to play jazz, jazz-fusion (I hate that term, but you know what I mean), most of the pop repertoire or ANYTHING whit a slight touch of Jazz, you MUST learn to recognize and play over the II V I Progression.

It appears in so many ways, mayor, minor, just the II-V without resolving into the I, as a chain of II-V's (each in a different key).
We could say that there are four "Main" II V I progressions, which when altering or substituting the V chord, give birth to other interesting variations.

These "Main" II V I progressions are:

IIm7 V7 IMaj7

IIm7 bII7 IMaj7 *

IIm7(b5) V7(b9) Im7

IIm7(b5) V7(b9) IMaj7

The first thing you should learn, is that generally speaking, the root motion of the II V I follows a fourths motion (Except for * Where the V7 is substituted by bII7, its Tritone substitution).

Other variation of this progression are produced by substituting the V7 for a V7 from another mode, for example, instead of V7, you play V7#5 or V7alt.
Another way to change the progression is substituting the V7 for its tritone substitution (bII7) or VII7.

Am7 - D7 - GMaj7

That is a II-V-I in the key of G Major.
Here you can see that each of the roots of the chords (not necessarily the "voicing") it's a fourth interval above its preceding chord.

This is the same in every key, of course, so I would recommend you to memorize these root movements in all 12 keys, but not only "visually", learn to hear them too, to identify them by ear in every chord inversion.

The amount of literature about the II V I progression is HUGHE, and I encourage you to seek out this material so you can apply that knowledge to this practical Guide too.

More important is though, to transcribe as much music as possible where this progression (and all others I'm giving you on this guide) is present, and then play those phrases and licks over the exercises I'll give you later in this book, and then transform then into your own.

I will give you a couple of simple exercises you can start practicing with. You MUST learn them all in all 12 keys though, so you have to transpose those ideas into the remaining keys and II-V-I variations.

Notice that I didn't write any accidentals at the beginning of each system, for teaching purposes I have written them in front of each note, so you can memorize the accidentals per chord too, very rarely a tune keeps its original key throughout its entire length, I find it vital to learn accidentals as they happen too, not just the key accidentals.

IIm7 V7 IMaj7

Let's start our II V I studies with the most basic progression: the II V I in a major key.
We have already talked about the different chord qualities from the major, natural minor, melodic minor and harmonic minor scales. So, you know that when we talk about the II V I of a major scale – of ANY major scale – the II is a **IIm7** chord, the V is a **V7** and, of course, the I is then a **IMaj7**.

In the key of C Major this is:

Dm7 G7 CMaj7
IIm7 **V7** **IMaj7**

So how do we practice it?

I'll start by saying this: you CAN practice by playing through the whole progression with the C Major scale, but that rarely results in interesting lines and won't help you become an advanced improviser. When you're improvising, you will hear melodies in your head. Play them. And don't ever worry if they're "just notes from the scale". But right now, we're talking about practicing. And this practice will help to free your creative mind when creating spontaneously (i.e. improvising).

What you should do though (besides practicing just with the scale), is practice playing the mode (and, in time, the modes) that corresponds to each chord of the progression.

So, on the IIm7, you will play the **Dorian Mode** off the root of that chord.

Dorian formula: **1 2 b3 4 5 6 b7**

Chord quality: **Minor 7**

Tensions: **9 11 13**

How to we do this when each chord is going by so fast?

This is where **Guide Tones**, the 3rd and 7th degrees of the chord, come in to play. So practice first by starting your phrases on either of those two notes.

So far so good, but we are going for a Dorian sound, not just the sound of a Minor 7 chord.

The Dorian Mode is the only minor scale that contains the 13th (major 6th of the scale) and the minor 7th. In the other minor scales, you either see the 13th joined by a major 7th, or the minor 7th joined by a minor 6th (remember: b6 = b13).

So the best way to outline the Dorian sound is to play the 13th in your phrases over the IIm7 chord.

On the V7 you will play the **Mixolydian Mode** off the root of the given chord.

Mixolydian formula: **1 2 3 4 5 6 b7**

Chord quality: **Dominant 7**

Tensions: **9 13**

On this particular V7, we do not encounter any altered tensions such as the b5, #5, b9 or #9. So including its guide tones, the 3rd and 7th, is the safest bet.

On the **IMaj7** chord, you will play the **Ionian Mode**, also known as the **Major Scale**.

Ionian Formula (the mother of ALL formulas: **1 2 3 4 5 6 7**

Chord quality: **Major 7**

Tensions:　　**9 13**

Here are some ideas to play around with.

The first is the one many beginning improvisers use to start studying scales over chord changes.
Play the scale in 16th notes up from the root of each chord.
It is a good way to start practicing your modes, too. I've seen many jazz masters practice like this before going on stage to this very day. It's an all-around good habit to incorporate into your routine.

Example 1.

The second example is one of those things you should do every day, like sleeping and breathing. It consists of playing the arpeggios of each chord in every inversion. Not only does this perfectly outline the harmony, helping your ears get accustomed to the overall sound of the progression, but it also makes you very proficient at "hitting the right notes" when improvising. You would be surprised how many jazz lines are based somehow on chord arpeggios. I don't think I'd be exaggerating when I said 90%.

If you have never practiced this, I recommend you start by playing every arpeggio up from its root over each chord. Like this:

When you feel comfortable with this, start practicing each chord in all of its inversions.
Let's take a look at the arpeggios played up from the 3rd (first inversion)

Again, when playing from the third is comfortable (i.e. when you can play this, fast, slow, with swing, shuffle, etc.), start playing the arpeggios from the 5th (second inversion):

And then from the 7th (third inversion):

Once you can play all of this decently (at any tempo, but with NO mistakes), start to practice connecting the arpeggios. We do this by starting at any note of the arpeggio, BUT instead of starting the next arpeggio in the same inversion as the previous one, we start the next one with the note closest possible note to the one we just finished playing.

Take a look at these variations of each of the previous examples:

Starting (the first arpeggio) on the root:

As you can see, we start the G7 arpeggio from the 3rd (B).
It is the closest note from C – the last note we play from the Dm7 arpeggio. C and B are just a half step from each other.
Notice though, that we want to keep a constant 8th note rhythm. So if the closest note from the previous one is THE SAME NOTE (a common tone between both arpeggios), we do not repeat it. If we did, it would sound like a "double step" – and it IS. But for the purpose of this practice routine, we want to avoid it – it gives us some kind of "rest"; a millisecond to "think".
While this is not a bad thing while improvising and having fun (I constantly play double steps and I DO love them), it is not so good for getting the harmony into your fingers and ears.

Now let's look at the next example starting the arpeggio on the 3rd scale degree:

Here, the last note of the first arpeggio is D, the root of Dm7. It is also the 5th of G7. Instead of repeating it at the start of G7, we play F, which is just a minor 3rd away from D. We could have started the G7 arpeggio with B as it's also a minor third away from D. On top of that, it's a guide tone (we love those). The only reason I chose not to start the arpeggio on B is because I didn't want to start the G7 arpeggio on the same scale degree as the Dm7 arpeggio. Besides, F is also a guide tone of G7 (and we LOVE those, remember?).

Starting on the 5th degree now:

One thing I also wanted to show you with this example is that on the CMaj7 arpeggio, I made a leap between the 5th (G) and the 7th (B). When practicing arpeggios, you don't necessarily have to play them up and back down again. While on the same chord/arpeggio, you can play the notes in any manner you want and should practice that as well. I only recommend that you start to practice your arpeggios going note by note without leaping to get them into your fingers first. Once you've achieved that, doing anything else with them is easier.

Now the last example, starting on the 7th degree of the first chord (3rd inversion)

There are INFINITE possibilities of how to practice arpeggios, for example, apply the same principles and practice this in 6/8, 12/8, etc.

Some ideas to help you write your own exercises:

1 - Play all arpeggios ascending only.

2 - Play all arpeggios descending only.

3 - Never play the root.

4 - Never play the 5th.

5 - Play the first two notes descending and the second two notes ascending on the first chord and the other way around on the next chord.

6 - The opposite of 5.

7 - etc., etc…

Now that you know what to do with your arpeggios and scales, lets combine them on each chord in order to squeeze the most out of them

The third practice example combines the notes from the Dm7 Arpeggio (D F A C) with the 6th degree of the scale, in this case B.

Example 3.

Notice that the phrase starts with a guide tone, the b3 of Dm7 (F).
The 13th (remember 13th = 6th), B, is played on a strong beat followed by the 7th of the chord, C, on an upbeat; this leads very smoothly into the D, the root, on a strong beat.

The first four notes of this phrase give you everything you need to get that Dorian sound – two guide tones and the 13th. You could also use this four-note idea to play on the IIm7 chords you encounter that are just half a bar long. In any case, it is a really good lick to play on your IIm7's.

The fourth example is one that EVERYONE should know. It's a typical jazz pattern which has survived for decades in the repertoire of many jazz masters.

It consists of playing the root of the chord, followed by its 9th, 3rd and 5th.
It is known as the "1 2 3 5 cell" or "1 2 3 5 **digital pattern**".

There are many **note Cells.** Every number refers to a degree of the scale or mode you are playing. The numbers are adapted to the scale too. For example, if you are playing the Locrian Mode (1 b2 b3 4 5 b6 b7) the 1 2 3 5 cell becomes "1 b2 b 3 b5" for that mode.

The important think to keep in mind though, is that the cell is still just the 1 2 3 5 degrees of any scale.

common Note Cells:

Four notes	Eight notes
1 2 3 1	1 2 3 4 5 3 2 1
1 2 3 5	1 2 3 4 5 7 6 5
1 3 5 3	1 5 3 2 1 2 3 5

Of course, you can invent your own note cells. 1 2 1 3, for example. Why not?

In this example, I applied a 1 2 3 5 note cell to the IIm7 and the V7 chords, which leads into a descending C major scale starting on its 3rd (again, we love guide tones).

It also shows another way to accent the 3rd as a guide tone. Notice that before playing the 3rd, the notes are a 2nd from one other (1 to 2 and 2 to 3), but when we reach the 3rd we leap up to the 5th. Our ears detect that 3rd interval between the 3rd and the 5th of the chord right away, and we immediately perceive the arpeggio of the chord.

In this case, by going straight to the 5th after the 3rd, we can start the pattern for the next chord smoothly, descending a 2nd into the root of the next chord.

Notice, too, that passing from the 5th of the V7 (D) chord into the 3rd of the IMaj7 (E) is extremely smooth.

Example 4.

In any case, your end goal should be to write your own lines. But to get you started, I've written some simple ideas for you to practice on the next page. There is a catch though: Each example its written in a different key. It's up to you to transpose each idea into all 12 keys.
And trust me, doing this work yourself will elevate your playing to a whole new level.

Also remember to listen to the masters, transcribe what you like from them and apply everything in this guide to them. Coltrane and Parker have some amazing II V I lines... just saying.

IIm7 V7 IMaj7

Sergio R. Klein

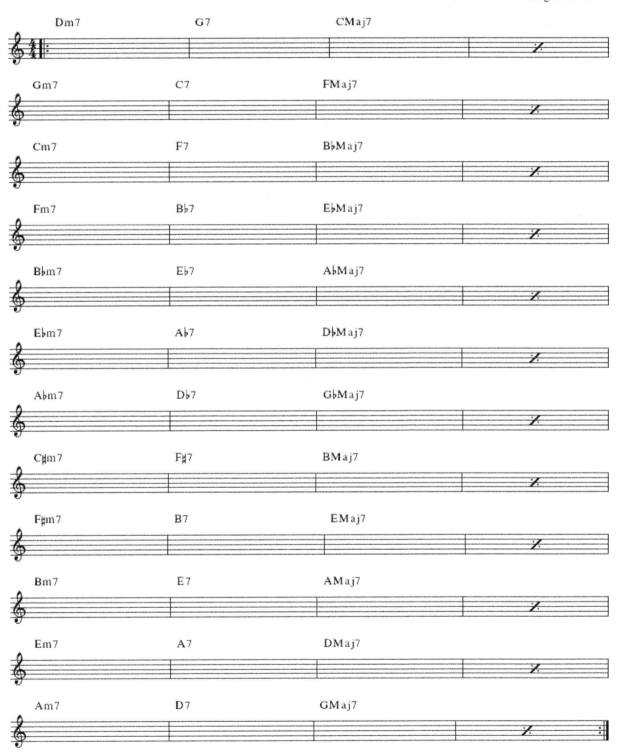

How to Master Chord Changes and Harmony

71

IIm7(b5) V7(b9) Im7

This is the first minor II V I progression we will look into. It is generally analyzed as a harmonic minor progression: the IIm7(b5) chord is, in this case, the second degree of harmonic minor and the V7(b9) is the fifth degree of harmonic minor.

Oddly enough, things get a bit "weird" on the Im7 chord. As you know, the harmonized harmonic minor scale's first degree is actually a minor triad with a major seventh. It spells mMaj7 or -Maj7.

The ImMaj7 is used, but to say it appears in 20% of our western repertoire would be almost an exaggeration. It is perhaps less than that. Jazz players replace the ImMaj7 for a "regular" minor chord; a m7 or m6 chord.

When you start to practice this progression, you can use three general approaches:

The "**arpeggio approach**": play each chord's arpeggio on each chord to start assimilating the sound and getting it into your fingers. Play one and two octave arpeggios; three octaves if your instrument allows it.

Start at the root of each chord, then on the 3rd, 5th and 7th.

Once you have done that, practice in the same way you did while learning the major II V I, and start connecting the arpeggios by starting the next one on the closest available note.

The "**key centered**" approach: play **harmonic minor** through the whole progression. You can even get away with playing the major 7th on the Im7 chord. You must always remember that music happens in moments, don't get too tied to "bars", use your ears to make it work.

Another one is to practice by playing each chord's mode over each chord.

On the **IIm7(b5)**, use second degree of harmonic minor, **Locrian 6**

Formula: 1   b2   b3   4   b5   6   b7   1

On the **V7(b9),** use fifth degree of harmonic minor, Phrygian Dominant

Formula: 1   b2   3   4   5   b6   b7   1

On the **Im7** is when things get confusing for most beginning improvisers due to a couple of things.

The 3rd of the V7(b9) chord is also the major 7th of the I chord. But when arriving at that I chord we actually have (most of the time) a m7 chord – a minor chord with a *minor* 7th. This opens up more options for the V7(b9) chord, but we'll get into that in a little bit.

So, what do we play on the Im7?

We actually have quite a few options...

The first thing you should practice, is playing I natural minor or the **Aeolian Mode** on the Im7. It sounds good, it is correct and you have no non-diatonic notes.

The Aeolian formula, as you know is: **1   2   b3   4   5   b6   b7   1**

A more "bluesy" approach would be to play a minor pentatonic scale. It has a different character than straight minor, but that could also be a good thing, depending on what you are playing and what "mood" you want your phrase to have.

A "modal" way to approach the IIm7(b5) V7(b9) Im7 is to use substitutions. For example, instead of playing the 2nd degree of harmonic minor on the IIm7(b5), you can play the sixth mode from melodic minor.

In the key of C Harmonic Minor, Dm7(b5) is its II, but Dm7(b5) is also the 6th mode of **F Melodic Minor**. So instead of playing Locrian on the II, you could play Locrian 2.

Formula of **Locrian 2**:   **1   2   b3   4   b5   b6   b7   1**

This sounds really good in my opinion, a bit "jazzier".

On the V7(b9) we can also play an altered scale; in other words; 7th degree of Melodic Minor or the Superlocrian Mode.

If the progression was in the key of C, this would mean a G7(b9). Instead of playing it as 5th degree of C Harmonic Minor, we use the 7th mode of Ab Melodic Minor:
G **Superlocrian** aka: G **Altered**.

The **Altered/Superlocrian** formula: **1   b2   b3   b4   b5   b6   b7   1**

This one sounds so good! I really love it. It is also really cool on paper: b4 sounds actually like a major 3rd. That plus the b7 are the guide tones of the dominant chord. On top of those two, you have every non-essential tone (i.e. tension) altered. What an amazing tool, wouldn't you say?

On the Im7 (or Im6) we can also play the Melodic Minor scale.

While the major 7th from the scale could present some trouble for the improviser, it adds so much in terms of general sound and color. It's used a lot in jazz; so much that we are quite accustomed to hearing it. Just avoid resolving your phrases into that Maj7 and you will be OK. As I said before, don't get too tied to "bars": music happens in "moments".

Let's sum up what we've talked about so far:

1) You can play the **Harmonic Minor** scale through the whole progression

2) On **IIm7(b5)** you can play:

- Half diminished arpeggio: **1 b3 b5 b7**

- **Locrian 6 Mode** (second mode of harmonic minor),

  formula: 1   b2   b3   4   b5   6   b7   1

- **Locrian 2 Mode** (sixth mode of melodic minor)

formula: 1   2   b3   4   b5   b6   b7   1

3) On **V7(b9)** you can play:

- Dominant 7th Arpeggio: **1 3 5 b7**

- **Phrygian Dominant Mode** (5th mode of harmonic minor)

  formula: 1   b2   3   4   5   b6   b7   1

- **Superlocrian/Altered Scale** (7th mode of melodic minor)

formula: 1   b2   b3   b4   b5   b6   b7   1

4) On **Im7** (or **Im6**) you can play:

- m7 Arpeggio: **1 b3 5 b7**

- m6 Arpeggio: **1 b3 5 6**

- **Minor Pentatonic** Scale: 1 b3 4 5 b7

- **Harmonic Minor** Scale

  formula: 1   2   b3   4   5   b6   7   1

- **Melodic Minor** Scale

  formula: 1   2   b3   4   5   6   7   1

One important thing here: I *know* it is a lot of information, scales and arpeggios to memorize, practice and think about. You must also know that you **don't** have to practice EVERYTHING right from the beginning.

Start simple: practice the variations which feel more natural to your ears or fingers. With time, you will eventually learn them all and you will also learn to incorporate everything into your own language.

Be disciplined and work **consistently** (!!!) EVERY DAY and you will see results pretty soon.

Enjoy learning, create your own phrases based on what you have learned so far and keep adding to the solid base of knowledge you're building.

How to practice:

1) <u>Arpeggios</u>:

- Play each arpeggio starting on the root of each chord.
- Play each arpeggio starting on the 3rd of each chord
- Play each arpeggio starting on the 5th of each chord
- Play each arpeggio starting on the 7th of each chord

-Start the first arpeggio of the progression starting on the root and then connect it to the next arpeggio in the progression by playing the closest available note.

example:

- Repeat the idea, but start on a different voice of the arpeggio each time.

Create as many variations as you want to, remember also that it is not necessary to play an arpeggio in consecutive intervals. You can jump to any note of the arpeggio while playing on one chord:

- Use rhythmic patterns too:

- Create your own arpeggio-based licks, phrases and motives through modal interchange and transposition, apply them to each chord and progression you learn.

- Practice in all the octaves your instrument allows (stringed instruments should practice this in all positions)

2) <u>Scales:</u>

- Play one scale for each chord, starting from the root and in ascending motion:

D Locrian 6   G Phrygian Dominant   C Natural Minor

- Start from the root and descend through the scale:

D Locrian 6   G Phrygian Dominant   C Harmonic Minor

- Apply the same idea, but starting from one of the guide tones (3rd and 7th, remember?)

D Locrian 2   G altered (G Superlocrian)   C Melodic Minor

- Do the same, but now connect the different scales by starting the next one at the closest available note (without repeating common notes):

D Locrian 2   Galt.   C Melodic Minor

- Practice the scales using note cells/digital patterns:

Four notes	Eight notes
1 2 3 1	1 2 3 4 5 3 2 1
1 2 3 5	1 2 3 4 5 7 6 5
1 3 5 3	1 5 3 2 1 2 3 5

- **You can also apply ANY scale exercise you know, including all of the above, to ALL chord progressions in this book or any other progression you may encounter**.

The more you practice like this – concentrated and relaxed – not letting yourself get discouraged by the amount of work ahead of you, the easier the learning of the next step becomes. Stay focused on what you are doing **right now** (for some students, this is the hardest thing to do).

Never forget that learning an instrument is a process whose success depends almost exclusively on how consistently you work. You have to teach your body, ears, brain and fingers to work together on every new challenge.
It is really simple in the end: keep practicing intelligently and consistently, you **will** get there.

IIm7(b5) V7(b9) Im7

Sergio R. Klein

How to Master Chord Changes and Harmony

78

IIm7(b5) V7(b9) IMaj7

As you can see, this progression is almost the same as the previous one. The only difference is that instead of resolving the V7(b9) into a ImMaj7, it resolves into a IMaj7.

When this happens, we call it a "deceptive resolution".

We frequently encounter many deceptive resolutions in the western repertoire, so I dedicated a little chapter to that in the theory section of this book.

For the time being, we will concentrate solely on this one: minor II V I resolving into a IMaj7.

To practice this one, we will use all the options we had for the first two chords from the previous cadence (that's IIm7(b5) V7(b9) Im7 for those of you who skipped that one).

For the **IMaj7** chord use the **Lydian Mode.** You could, in theory, use the major scale/Ionian Mode too, but almost no one would give up that juicy #11 from the Lydian Mode, so it happens very rarely. But I have to mention it, because it is a valid option. Just not as exciting as the Lydian Mode.

I will sum it up for you, no worries:

1) You can play **Harmonic minor** scale through the first two chords. Lydian Mode for the IMaj7.

2) On **IIm7(b5)** you can play:

- Half diminished arpeggio: **1 b3 b5 b7**

- **Locrian 6 mode** (second mode of harmonic minor),

formula: **1   b2   b3   4   b5   6   b7   1**

- **Locrian 2 mode** (sixth mode of melodic minor)

formula: **1   2   b3   4   b5   b6   b7   1**

3) On **V7(b9)** you can play:

- Dominant 7th Arpeggio: **1 3 5 b7**

- **Phrygian Dominant mode** (5th mode of harmonic minor)

formula: **1   b2   3   4   5   b6   b7   1**

- **Superlocrian/altered scale** (7th mode of melodic minor)

formula: **1   b2   b3   b4   b5   b6   b7   1**

4) On the **IMaj7**, as I said before, use the Lydian Mode:

formula: **1   2   3   #4   5   6   7   1**

Start practicing with the ones that sound the best to you first. When you nail those, practice the others if you like.

I recommend you start with the "non-altered" options: Locrian 6 for the half-diminished, Phrygian Dominant for the V7(b9) and Lydian for the IMaj7.

Get those sounds into your ears first – it makes it easier to assimilate the "altered" ones; Locrian 2 for the IIm7(b5) and Superlocrian/Altered for the V7(b9).

The practice method is the same as for the other II V I we have been practicing this entire time:

1) Arpeggios:

- Play each arpeggio starting on the root of each chord
- Play each arpeggio starting on the 3rd of each chord
- Play each arpeggio starting on the 5th of each chord
- Play each arpeggio starting on the 7th of each chord

2) Scales:

- Play one scale per chord, starting from the root in an ascending motion.
- Start from the root and descend through the scale.
- Apply the same ideas, but starting from one of the guide tones (the 3rd and 7th).
- Do the same (ascending and descending), but now connect the different scales by starting the next scale at the nearest note possible without repeating common notes.
-Practice the scales using note cells/digital patterns:

Four notes	Eight notes
1 2 3 1	1 2 3 4 5 3 2 1
1 2 3 5	1 2 3 4 5 7 6 5
1 3 5 3	1 5 3 2 1 2 3 5

IIm7(b5) V7(b9) IMaj7

Sergio R. Klein

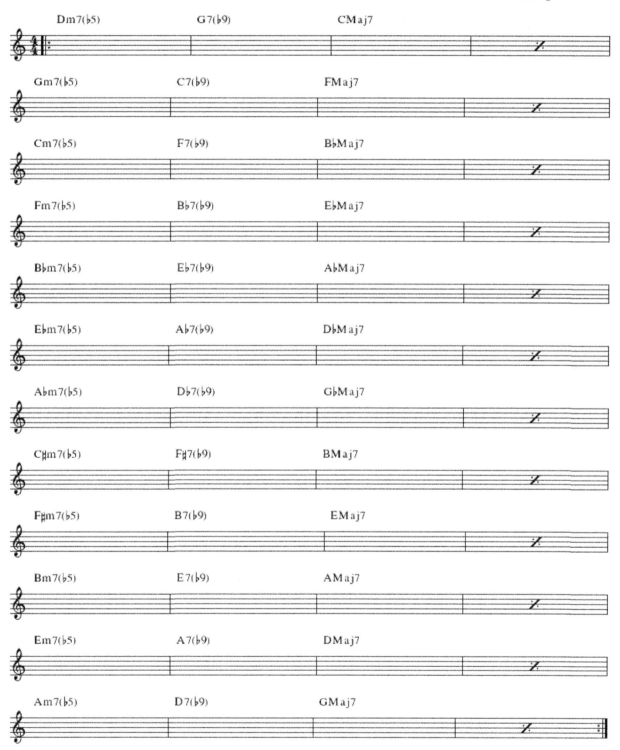

IIm7 bII7 IMaj7

Here we have a variation of the IIm7 V7 IMaj7 progression. It is still a "Major Scale progression", because the function of the chords gravitates around and resolves on the tonic chord of a major scale: IMaj7

The only – but very important – difference here is that instead of using V7, we replace it with its tritone substitution: **bII7**.

We have already talked a lot about the tritone substitution in the chapter on theory, so you already know how and why it works so well.

The IIm7 bII7 IMaj7 progression is really easy to identify by ear, due to the half-step descending movement of the chords' roots.

Let's start practicing this progression. First, instead of playing the Mixolydian mode over the bII7, we play the **4th mode of Melodic Minor**, better known as the **Lydian Dominant Mode.**

Its formula, as you already know, is **1 2 3 #4 5 6 b7**, and it has the tensions **9 #11** and **13**.

That is where the name comes from, its chord has a Dominant 7 quality, but the 11th is raised a half step, as in the Lydian mode – simple as that.

On the **IIm7**, we play the **Dorian Mode**, just like we would over the non-altered IIm7 V7 IMaj7. And on the IMaj7, we play the **Ionian Mode**.

So, to review:

on **IIm7** use **Dorian mode**: 1 2 b3 4 5 6 b7; tensions: 9 11 13

on **bII7** use **Lydian Dominant mode**: 1 2 3 #4 5 6 b7; tensions: 9 #11 13

on **IMaj7** use the **Major Scale** also known as **Ionian Mode**: 1 2 3 4 5 6 7; tensions: 9 13

Notice that now, you can't play a single major scale over the entire progression as with the unaltered IIm7 V7 IMaj7. That's s because the bII7 chord is a non-diatonic chord.

To start practicing this progression, apply everything you did on the IIm7 V7 IMaj7 progression and simply adjust the arpeggios and scales for the bII7.

Practice Tips:

- Play each mode starting from the root using 8ths and 16ths

- Play each mode starting on a guide tone (3rd and 7th)

- Play arpeggios in each inversion (starting with the root, 3rd, 5th and 7th of the chord) on each chord of the progression.

- Start by playing the IIm7 arpeggio in any inversion and connect it to the bII7 arpeggio at its closest note, then connect the bII7 to the IMaj7 in the same manner.

- Apply any four- and eight-note **digital pattern** (note cells) you know to each chord of the progression. I suggest you start with the **1 2 3 5** pattern.

- Use Modal Interchange to turn any Mixolydian lick or phrase into Lydian Dominant, and play it on the bII7.

IIm7 bII7 IMaj7

Sergio R. Klein

II V I
Scale Usage Guide

Sergio R. Klein

Dorian mode: 1   2   b3   4   5   6   b7

Mixolydian mode: 1   2   3   4   5   6   b7

Lydian mode: 1   2   3   #4   5   6   7

Locrian 6 mode: 1   b2   b3   4   b5   6   b7

Locrian 2 mode: 1   2   b3   4   b5   b6   b7

Phrygian Dominant mode: 1   b2   3   4   5   b6   b7

Superlocrian mode (alterede scale):   1   b2   b3   b4   b5   b6   b7

Aeolian mode: 1   2   b3   4   5   b6   b7

Melodic minor scale: 1   2   b3   4   5   6   7

Lydian Dominant mode: 1   2   3   #4   5   6   b7

Check out these II V I Phrases

inspired by some incredible musicians

Sergio R. Klein

Cycles

Introduction to Cycle Progressions

There are five progressions that occur very often in jazz and pop music. They are eight bars long, they start with the I chord and also end with two consecutive bars of the I chord. This is why they are commonly known as Cycle Progressions, as they "come back" to the I.

Do not confuse them with Turnarounds. Turnarounds end on a V7 and then go back to the beginning of the tune.

Do not mistake Cycle Progressions for the cycle of fifths, fourths, third, etc., either. Cycle Progressions are chord progressions and are built through a tension/resolution process. Often, they include very common cadences like the II V I at the end, for example.

They sound very different from each other for the most part, and each of them has something special going on.

One thing I really like about them is that the number of the bar doesn't determine which function the respective chord in that bar will have (except for bar number 1, 7 and 8. Those are I chords).

I opted to leave these Cycle Progressions for the end of the book. They use many mechanics, scales, tritone substitutions, secondary dominants, etc., that we needed to learn slowly in order not to get overwhelmed with a bunch of new information.

It is way easier to learn these mechanics and theory applications slowly and in a logical order and THEN mix them all up.

Here is a list of Cycle Progressions. We'll go into every one of them in detail in the following chapters.

Each dash represents a bar line:

Cycle 1: IMaj7 - III7(b9) - VIm7 - VI7(b13) - IIm7 - V7 - IMaj7 - IMaj7

Cycle 2: IMaj7 - VII7(b9,b13) - IMaj7 - VI7(b9,b13) - II7 - V7 - IMaj7

Cycle 3: IMaj7 - IV7(#11) - IIIm7 - bIII7(#11) - IIm7 - bII7(#11) - IMaj7

Cycle 4: IMaj7 - I7 - IVMaj7 - bVI(#11) - V7sus4 - bII7(#11) - IMaj7

Cycle 5: IMaj7 - bV7(#11) - IVMaj7 - bVII7(#11) - IMaj7 - V7 - IMaj7

Cycle 1:

IMaj7 - III7(b9) - VIm7 - VI7(b13) - IIm7 - V7 - IMaj7 - IMaj7

Let's begin our Cycle Progression studies with this one. I find that this cycle is a good one to practice to start up your day. It delves into the major, Harmonic Minor and Melodic Minor scales. It is easy to remember and easy on the ears too, partly because it has been used consistently in the western repertoire for many decades now.

Before we start studying this progression, I need to make a comment about musical context so you can better understand why we use the scales we use. I also do it to point out the fact that musical theory and language are always evolving, allowing for the surge of new elements, like scales/chord relationships, articulation, form, etc. This, in turn, gets absorbed by new musicians and audiences. After a while (and nowadays not a long while) they become part of our modern repertoire and open new possibilities for the future also.

Nowadays, there are many scales and arpeggios to choose from when playing over chords. Especially dominant chords. The use of this or that element depends mostly on how you want to mold your sound (i.e. if it should sound more "modern", "outside", "bluesy", "rock-ish", etc.)

Logically, we have more options now than musicians did 100 years ago. We, curious musicians, have always been testing and challenging our musical knowledge in order to discover something new and exciting to do with the tools we have learned so far.

This curiosity has allowed the surge of new music styles, harmonic tools, forms, rhythms and their interactions with each other consistently throughout music history so far.

Think about the blues for example. Many times, while playing and/or listening to the blues you have heard a minor scale being played over major chords consistently. And it hasn't even bothered you a little bit. A Minor Pentatonic Scale over a dominant seventh chord, or even a major triad, isn't something new. It doesn't sound dissonant or "wrong" to your ears. It probably sounds really nice actually.

Now think how this would have been received by the ears of a German composer in 1650. It would be unthinkable for him. It must have sounded horrible. In fact, that I7, IV7 and V7 in succession must have been an aberration for someone used to "preparing" the 7th of a V7 chord several bars before he even dared to write it.

I mean, even Claude Debussy was EXPELLED from the conservatory for adding tensions to his chords and moving away from traditional tonal music.

He sounded almost like a hard bop pianist in the 19th century!

What I meant to tell you with all of this is that the scales I give to you are not set in stone. They are the ones you MUST know, so you can then move on and experiment with other possibilities. They are the most "correct" ones, the ones nobody will complain about when you play in a hotel's restaurant.

Most importantly, though, they are the base, the "trampoline" for your future musical development.

I share this with you with two things that are really important to me in mind:

Although I tell you which scales go over which chords, how many bars this or that progression has, and how VITAL it is that you learn the things I share with you, you MUST keep challenging your ears, your mind, your ideas and ego.
If you find a new scale that sounds good to you when play it over a certain chord, PLAY IT.

Try to figure out WHY it sounds good to you. Is it the new tensions that are exciting your ears? Is it the fact that these new tensions make the resolution into the next chord sound more "surprising", or is it just the sound? Maybe the register in which you played them on your instrument?

Ask yourself as many questions as you can. Challenge what you already know. Ask your fellow musicians. Play, play, play and LISTEN.

That being said, let me refresh some information we discussed in the chapter "The Right Scale over the Right Chord" in the theory unit of this book.

The primary method use to identify which scale to play over any given chord is quite simple.

First, we identify which key the overall progression is in.

To demonstrate this, let's pick this first cycle progression and play it in the key of C major:

CMaj7 - E7 - Am7 - A7 - Dm7 - G7 - CMaj7 - CMaj7

CMaj7 on the first bar is of course our I from the C major scale. No need to comment on that.

Then comes an E7 chord. Secondary dominant of Am7, the VI from C major.
We know though, that the third degree of C major is E**m7**, so if we play E Phrygian (third mode of the major scale) over E7 it won't work too well... and that's an understatement.

So what do we do? Simple. We just need to alter the note or notes from the scale we'd use to play over the Em7 chord to make it work over an E7 chord.

Em7 Phrygian: E   F   G   A   B   C   D
                   1   b3   5   b7

As you can see, the only note we need to alter is the b3. We need to raise it a half step in order to get an E7 chord. To complete the scale, we just fill in the space between the chord tones with the rest of the notes from the original scale. The resulting scale is the following:

E7 Phrygian Dominant: E   F   G#   A   B   C   D
                             1   (b9)   3   11   5 (b13) b7

You may have noticed the b9th. Because we don't need to alter the F note to get the G7 chord, we simply don't. That is why we don't play the Mixolydian Mode over a III7 chord. It is less desirable because we would need to alter three notes. Mixolydian has a natural 6th and a natural 9th AND it's a major mode.

So which scale has every note in common with C major, except for G#?

That's right: A Harmonic Minor. And E7(b9) is the chord built off the 5th degree of A Harmonic Minor.

A Harmonic Minor: A B C D E F G#

That's why we choose to play Phrygian Dominant, or "5th mode of Harmonic Minor" over III7 chords. It's the most logical (and traditional) option.

Tip: Altering less notes helps you best outline the harmony in your melodic lines.
Let's move on to the next chord, VIm7. In the key of C Major this is Am7. Nothing new here. 6th mode of the Major Scale is the Aeolian Mode, so that's what we play here:

A Aeolian: A   B   C   D   E   F   G
                1   2 b3   4   5 b6 b7

Then we have another non-diatonic chord: VI7.

Same method as before: we alter just the note from the scale we need to in order to change the original chord from a VIm7 into a VI7.

The result is A Mixolydian b6, 5th mode of D Melodic Minor:

                A   B C# D   E   F   G
                1   2   3   4   5 b6 b7

This is the best option. Not only do we alter just one note from the original key, but the b13 of the chord (b6 = b13) anticipates the b3 of the next chord, in this case F – the guide tone and flat 3rd degree of Dm7. Not to mention that Mixolydian b6 sounds terrific on its own.

To continue with the progression, we have a IIm7 V7 IMaj7 followed by another bar of IMaj7.

Since all of those are diatonic chords, we just play their relative modes from the parent key. In the key of C major, these are:

Dm7 Dorian   D   E   F   G   A   B   C
                         1   2 b3   4   5   6 b7

G7 Mixolydian   G   A   B   C   D   E   F
                         1   2   3   4   5   6 b7

CMaj7 Ionian   C   D   E   F   G   A   B
                         1   2   3   4   5   6   7

As I said: the IMaj7 - III7(b9) - VIm7 - VI7(b13) - IIm7 - V7 - IMaj7 - IMaj7 cycle is really good to start your daily practice session.

It includes the three main scales of our harmonic vocabulary – the major, melodic minor and harmonic minor scales – all interacting in the same harmonic context.

You know how to practice already, but a short reminder is always welcome:

1) Arpeggio approach: arpeggios up and down, starting on each inversion using 8ths 16ths, triplets, and rhythm patterns; connecting each arpeggio to the next, targeting and resolving into the guide tones, etc.

2) Scale approach: Play the corresponding scale over each chord ascending and descending starting each scale on the root or one of the guide tones. Resolve into the next scale by starting it at the nearest note possible or at one of the guide tones, etc.

Also, apply rhythmic patterns. You can also try to limit yourself to play just one interval: play through the scale just using 4ths or 6ths, etc.

3) Digital Patterns: Play any of the given (eventually all plus your own) Digital Patterns on each chord.

Four notes	Eight notes
1 2 3 1	1 2 3 4 5 3 2 1
1 2 3 5	1 2 3 4 5 7 6 5
1 3 5 3	1 5 3 2 1 2 3 5

4) Phrases and Licks: Play whatever lick or phrase you have transcribed or written over every chord. Combine them as you like and transforming them through transposition and modal interchange, allowing you to play each phrase over any chord.

Cycle 1

Eight Note Digital Pattern

Sergio R. Klein

CMaj7 · E7(b9) · IMaj7 · III7(b9)

Am7 · A7(b13) · VIm7 · VI7(b13)

Dm7 · G7 · IIm7 · V7

CMaj7 · CMaj7(#11) · IMaj7 · IMaj7(#11)

Cycle 2:

IMaj7 - VII7(b9,b13) - IMaj7 - VI7(b13) - II7 - V7 - IMaj7

We talked a lot already about how to figure out which scale goes over which chord. I'm going to assume you have memorized that information by now and keep this one short.

First chord: **IMaj7**

Nothing new here: Ionian mode would be going "by the book", but the best sounding choice is, in my opinion, the Lydian mode. I don't think it is just my opinion...

Formula: you know those formulas already, let's move on.

Second chord: **VII7**

Also, nothing new, but people tend to forget. **VII7** uses <u>5th mode of Harmonic Minor</u>: the <u>Phrygian Dominant</u> Mode.

Formula: 1   b2   3   4   5   b6   b7

Why?

In the key of C:

Bm7(b5) Locrian =   B   C   <u>D</u>   E   <u>F</u>   G   A
                    1   b2   b3   4   b5   b6   b7

We need B7, so we raise D and F a half step:

B   C   <u>D#</u>   E   <u>F#</u>   G   A
1   b9   3   4   5   b6   b7 = Phrygian Dominant formula

This is also why the specific tensions of VII7 are the b9 and b13.

Next chord: **IMaj7**

Should I?... Really?

Next chord: **VI7**

Nothing new, but I'm going to explain it again anyway (Maybe you started reading the book on this page, who knows? Crazier things happen every second).

On **VI7** we play <u>5th mode of Melodic Minor</u>: the Mixolydian b6 Mode. I have to say, though, that you can use Phrygian Dominant here too. It sounds good and enough musicians have done so in the past, so go for it if you prefer it.

The best option <u>in my opinion</u> is Mixolydian b6; it sounds more interesting, jazzy and has actually more notes in common with the chord of the parent key of the progression. A win-win situation. Be a winner.

In the key of C:

Am7 Aeolian:	A	B	C	D	E	F	G
	1	2	b3	4	5	b6	b7

A7(b13) Mixolydian b6:	A	B	C#	D	E	F	G
	1	2	3	4	5	b6	b7

Next chord: **II7**

By now you are a **II7** expert and know that you should play Mixolydian mode here.

Its formula – 1   2   3   4   5   6   b7 – is the first thing you think about when you wake up in the morning (around noon?) and the last think you think about before you go to sleep… even if you don't admit it to your girlfriend or boyfriend, you know its true. You know…

Next chord: **V7**

Mixolydian Mode, because Mixolydian Mode! And also, because reasons!

Last chord: **IMaj7**

What a surprise… Major Scale: 1   2   3   4   5   6   7

I actually wrote it down just to annoy you.

Now, if you really want to sound **_amazing_**: play Lydian: 1   2   3   #4   5   6   b7

Playing the Lydian Mode at least five minutes a day increases your lifespan by approximately seven and a half years and makes you more attractive.

That is a proven fact.

Cycle 2
Two Different Four-Note Digital Pattern

Sergio R. Klein

Cycle 3:

IMaj7 - IV7(#11) - IIIm7 - bIII7(#11) - IIm7 - bII7(#11) - IMaj7

I really like this one. It just sounds beautiful. You can hear it also all over the western repertoire to this very day.

The scales we use for the diatonic chords are well known to you by now:
IMaj7 uses Ionian or Lydian, IIIm7 is Phrygian and IIm7 is, of course, Dorian. Nothing new there.

This progression is perfect to practice your Lydian Dominant chops, as this is the scale we use over IV7, bIII7 and bII7.

Let's go over the reasons why we use this scale one more time together.

In the key of C:

In C major, the 4th degree is FMaj7 Lydian. In this progression, however, the IV degree is presented as a IV7 chord. In C this would be F7. The only note we need to change then is the 7th; we lower it a half step:

F Lydian =		F	G	A	B	C	D	E
		1	2	3	#4	5	6	7

F Lydian Dominant =		F	G	A	B	C	D	Eb
		1	2	3	#4	5	6	b7

Let's do the same for bIII7 and bII7:

In the case of Eb7 (the bIII7 chord), the root is non-diatonic. If we change just that note and keep the rest of the notes diatonic to the original key, we soon realize that this is not enough to give us the Lydian Dominant:

Eb	F	G	A	B	C	D
1	2	3	#4	#5	6	7

We still need to lower the 7th and the 5th:

Eb	F	G	A	Bb	C	D	
1	2	3	#4	5	6	b7	= Lydian Dominant formula

Now let's turn that IIm7 into a bII7. In the key of C this would be Dm7 into Db7:

Dm7 Dorian =   D   E   F   G   A   B   C
                   1   2   b3   4   5   6   b7

You can tell that we will need to change almost every note of the scale in order to get that Db7. Let's see what happens:

              Db   Eb   F   G   Ab   Bb   Cb (B)
              1   2   3   #4   5   6   b7   = Lydian Dominant formula

I want to say though, that many players nowadays go for the Altered scale too. It is perfectly fine. It has a very interesting sound, but you will notice that your ears will want to resolve it a half step up instead of a half step down.

Typically, you will find that dominant chords that resolve a half step down use the Lydian Dominant mode. I will add a last chapter dedicated just to dominant chords at the end of the book. The options are many and I feel I have to outline them all for you.

There are many possibilities and I urge you to seek them all out and also experiment with your own ideas. I do, however, recommend you learn the most used scales first; the ones deeply rooted in our repertoire and eventually led to all the options we have today. If we continue to question our knowledge, we will have even more options in the future.

To summarize Cycle 3:

IMaj7: Major scale or Lydian mode

IV7(#11): Lydian Dominant mode

IIIm7: Phrygian mode

bIII7(#11): Lydian Dominant mode

IIm7: Dorian mode

bII7(#11): Lydian Dominant mode

IMaj7: Major scale or Lydian mode

Cycle 3
Eight-Note Digital Pattern 2

Sergio R. Klein

CMaj7   F7(#11)

1 2 3 4 - 5 7 6 5 etc...

IMaj7   IV7(#11)

Em7   Eb7(#11)

IIIm7   bIII7(#11)

Dm7   Db7(#11)

IIm7   bII7(#11)

CMaj7#11   CMaj7

IMaj7#11   IMaj7

Cycle 4:

IMaj7 - I7 - IVMaj7 - bVI(#11) - V7sus4 - bII7(#11) - IMaj7

If you take a close look at this progression, you will notice that there is one chord quality we haven't covered yet: the **7sus4**.

This is a chord where the major 3rd has been replaced by the 4th.
It sounds very cool and although it's been used for centuries in classical music (as part of **V7sus4 - V7 - I**), it always sounds modern and refreshing due to its suspended sound.

Maybe the most well-known example of the 7sus4 chord in jazz music is "Maiden Voyage" from Herbie Hancock. Do yourself an ENORMOUS favor and go listen to Herbie's music. It is a true treasure for any musician or music enthusiast out there.

Back to the topic at hand.

On this chord you have a couple of options: In theory, you can play the Mixolydian Mode over this chord, but making sure to avoid its 3rd as a resolution note.

The other option, and the most popular, is to play a major pentatonic scale up from the 7th of the chord.

For example: over G7sus4, play F major pentatonic.

	F	G	A	C	D
Major pentatonic formula:	1	2	3	5	6

This is the same as playing a minor pentatonic scale down a 4th (up a 5th is exactly the same) from the chord's root. You can also think about it like playing a minor pentatonic up from the 5th of the chord. In the end, it doesn't matter if you think down a 4th or up a 5th. They are just different ways of thinking about the very same notes.

Over G7sus4 play D minor pentatonic:

	D	F	G	A	C
Minor pentatonic formula:	1	b3	4	5	b7

As you can see, the notes are exactly the same, so choose the easiest "mental shortcut" for yourself and go practice it.

Now that we have talked about that, let's take a closer look into the other chords present in this progression.

The first chord: **IMaj7**

I think that by now we agree that the Major Scale and the lifespan-prolonging scale called the Lydian Mode go over this one, right?

Now, the second chord, **I7** is easy. We just have to change one note from the original key in order to get this chord quality.
We lower the 7th a half step. The result is quite obvious: the Mixolydian Mode.

1 2 3 4 5 6 b7

Moving on...

IVMaj7 is also no mystery for you at this point: Lydian Mode

1 2 3 #4 5 6 7

Next chord: **bVI7(#11)**

This one resolves a half step down. As we know, non-diatonic Dominant 7 chords which resolve a half step down use Lydian Dominant Mode, the mode which lets you feel the force around you.

1 2 3 #4 5 6 b7

Next chord: **V7sus4**

As we said before, you can play the Mixolydian Mode over this chord, if you avoid resolving your phrases on its major 3rd. I really recommend playing the Major Pentatonic up from the 7th of the chord, which is the same as playing the Minor Pentatonic up from the 5th of the chord. Whatever's easier for you to remember; the notes are the same. When you play these scales, you are actually playing the b7th, root, 9th, 4th and 5th of the V7sus chord.

Choose your destiny...

Major Pentatonic: 1   2   3   5   6

Minor Pentatonic: 1 b3   4   5   b7

The next chord is a wonderful bII7(#11), which as you have memorized by now, is the tritone substitution for V7. It resolves a half step down, uses the amazing Lydian Dominant Mode. And by using this scale over this chord, you become a little bit more awesome in the process, too. I swear it.

Totally redundant, but I can't help it somehow:

1 2 3 #4 5 6 b7

Last chord: **IMaj7**

MAJOR SCALE: 1 2 3 4 5 6 7

For the last bar, I would definitely go for Lydian though.

Lydian Mode: 1 2 3 #4 5 6 7

As if you didn't know that one already...

Cycle 4
Four-Note Digital Pattern 3 and 2(variation)

Sergio R. Klein

Cycle 5

IMaj7 - bV7(#11) - IVMaj7 - bVII7(#11) - IMaj7 - V7 - IMaj7

In this progression, we have only two non-diatonic chords: **bV7** and **bVII7**.

IMaj7, IVMaj7 and V7 are all diatonic and use the corresponding modes:

Use the **Ionian Mode** for the **IMaj7** on the first, fifth and seventh bar. On the eight bar, you can use the **Lydian mode**.

The **IVMaj7** uses **Lydian** and the **V7** uses **Mixolydian**.

Let's focus on the <u>non-diatonic</u> chords now.

As you know, **bV7** is the tritone substitution of I7. This chord is the secondary dominant of **IVMaj7**.

As usual, the **bV7** chord resolves a half step down into **IV**, in this case **IVMaj7** (sometimes, as we have seen before, the IV can be present as a IV7).

The scale we use in this case is Lydian Dominant. Its formula is:

$$1 \quad 2 \quad 3 \quad \#4 \quad 5 \quad 6 \quad b7$$

We have already talked about why this scale fits perfectly here.

Let's look at why we also use **Lydian Dominant** over the **bVII7** chord.

Dominant chords resolving a whole step up is really common in contemporary music. This phenomenon is everywhere. I have even heard it in electronic music and trip-hop, not to mention "fusion" bands, Pat Metheny, etc... it has been a "thing" for many years already.

Let's get into the "math" of it, so you also understand why it actually works.

If we were to resolve a Bb7 into a CMaj7, the notes we need for that chord are

Bb7 =	Bb	D	F	Ab
	1	3	5	b7

Now let's fill in the notes we need to complete the scale with notes from key of C major:

Bb	C	D	E	F	G	Ab
1	2	3	#4	5	6	b7

Combining the notes of the Bb7 chord with the notes of the C Major scale gives us the formula for the Bb Lydian Dominant Mode.

You've got to **LOVE** harmony!

Cycle 5
Combining Different Digital Patterns

Sergio R. Klein

Rhythm Changes

Rhythm Changes

"Rhythm Changes" is a 32 bar AABA form, consisting of four eight-bars sections. The chord changes from the jazz standard "I Got Rhythm" are the ones upon which the "Rhythm Changes" progression is based. That's where this progression got its name from. The changes on the original version of "I Got Rhythm" are a bit different from the ones we most commonly use today.

Many musicians during the Bebop era didn't want to pay royalties to the Gershwins (the brothers Ira and George Gershwin wrote the original "I Got Rhythm") for recording and performing that song. They still really liked the tune's chord changes and, as you probably know, melodies can be copyrighted, but chord changes can't.

To avoid paying royalties, these musicians started writing their own melodies over the changes. This practice of writing melodies over chord changes from other songs became the basis of many classics of jazz, including *Anthropology* and *Dexterity* from the great Charlie Parker and many others from that era.
Composers also started using Rhythm Changes as a section within the larger form of their compositions.
They would write an A section and then use the Rhythm Changes progression as the bridge of their own tune.
Often the bridge section in Rhythm Changes has no set melody and is left open for improvisations, as in *Oleo* by Sonny Rollins.

The **A** section of the Rhythm Changes is a **I -VI7 - IIm7 - V7** progression played twice, followed by a four bar **I - I7 - IV - IVm6 - I - V7 - I** progression. Each bar contains two chords.

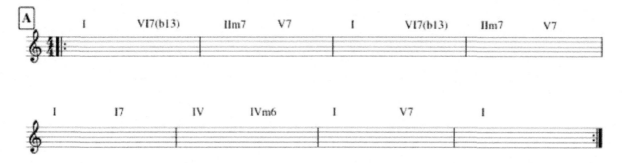

The **B** section or "**Bridge**" is a series of dominant sevenths chords. The roots of these chords follow the circle of fourths, also known as the "Ragtime Progression". In this section, each chord is sustained for two bars. This gives us the feeling that we are moving to a new key center. At the end of the bridge we find the diatonic V7 which resolves into the next section.

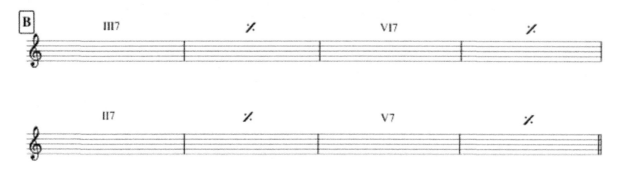

Then the **A** section returns, but played just once. The complete form looks like this:

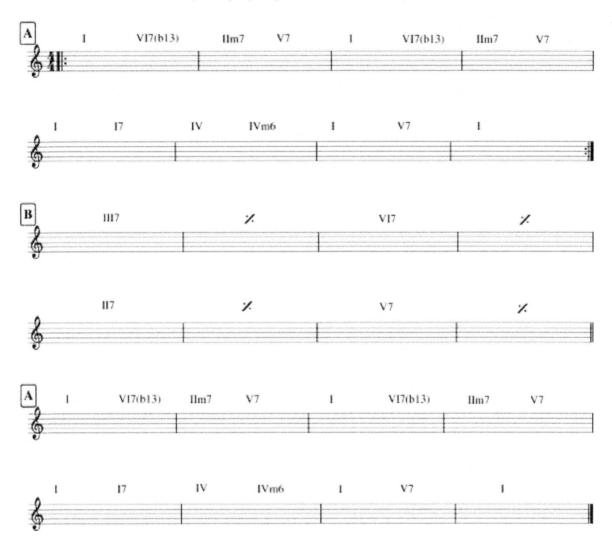

So, what do we play over these chords?

On the **diatonic chords,** we play their correspondent mode:

I = <u>Major scale/Ionian mode</u>: 1 2 3 4 5 6 7

VIm (it can also be present instead of VI7) = <u>Aeolian mode</u>: 1 2 b3 4 5 b6 b7

IIm7 = <u>Dorian mode</u>: 1 2 b3 4 5 6 b7

V7 = <u>Mixolydian mode</u>: 1 2 3 4 5 6 b7

IV = <u>Lydian mode</u>: 1 2 3 #4 5 6 7

Over the **non-diatonic** chords, we play the following scales:

I7 = Mixolydian mode: 1   2   3   4   5   6   b7

VI7(b13) = 5th mode of melodic minor: 1 2 3 4 5 b6 b7

IVm6 = Melodic minor scale: 1 2 b3 4 5 6 7

IV7 (used in some variations instead of IVm6) = Lydian Dominant mode:

1 2 3 #4 5 6 b7

III7 = 5th mode of harmonic minor: 1 b2 3 4 5 b13 b7

So how do we know which scale to play over non-diatonic chords?

Non-diatonic chords have at least one non-diatonic note. In order to get the scale formula for that chord, the only thing we need to do is take the notes from the original key in which we are playing, and alter the notes which are different in the non-diatonic chord. Or, if you prefer, take all the notes from the non-diatonic chord, and then fill in with the diatonic notes from the original key.

For example:

We have a I7 chord. This is a non-diatonic chord. It contains a non-diatonic note, in this case a minor 7th.

In the key of C, CMaj7 is the first degree of the scale. In order for it to become C7, we need to lower B, its major 7th, a half step. This way we get the note Bb, the flatted 7th of C7.

We get the scale we need to play over this chord by adding the rest of the notes from the original key:

C D E F G A Bb
<u>1</u> 2 <u>3</u> 4 <u>5</u> 6 <u>b7</u>

The underlined notes are the notes from the C7 chord, and the rest; D, F, and A, are the notes we took from the original key to complete the scale.

The resulting formula is 1   2   3   4   5   6   b7 : the Mixolydian Mode formula.

This is why we play the <u>Mixolydian</u> Mode over **I7** chords.

To figure out which scale goes over **IV7**, we use the same method:

The diatonic 4th degree of a major scale is, as you know, **IVMaj7**.
Again, the only thing we need to do is to lower the 7th one half step.

Keep in mind that the 4th mode of the major scale is the Lydian Mode. Its formula is:

1 2 3 #4 5 6 7

After lowering the 7th a half step, the formula changes to:

1 2 3 #4 5 6 <u>b7</u>

The famous Lydian Dominant Mode; beloved by jazz musicians. It is the 4th mode of the melodic minor scale. This means that if we are playing the rhythm changes progression in the key of C, the scale we'll play over the **IV7** chord, F7 in this case, is the F Lydian Dominant Mode, 4th mode of C Melodic Minor.

Over IVm6 we use Melodic Minor.

1 2 b3 4 5 6 7

A minor scale with a major 6th and a major 7th: Melodic Minor, the perfect match.

There is another option, however, and it is – diatonically speaking – even more fitting.

If we take the original Lydian Scale: 1 2 3 #4 5 6 7 and lower the 3rd so we get the **IVm6** chord, we get the following formula:

1 2 b3 #4 5 6 7

That is not a Melodic Minor Scale. It is in fact the 4th mode of Harmonic Minor... so why use Melodic Minor over **IVm6**? Wouldn't it be better to use the 4th mode of Harmonic Minor? It does include the #4 after all.

The answer is pretty simple: it sounds "better"

Now, "better" is a subjective term at best, but traditionally, jazz musicians try to avoid the Harmonic Minor scale. The augmented 2nd between its 6th and 7th degrees tends to sound forced or "too harsh" when phrasing and it can be very tricky to make it sound good and/or interesting. It just screams "HARMONIC MINOR!!!". It isn't a very subtle sound.

Over the years, musicians have used the Melodic Minor so much over **IVm6**, that we are now used to it. The scale somehow sounds "better" to our western-trained ears.

Never forget that culture plays a major role in what we consider to be "good" sounding.
Take the Blues, for example. A musical form which most of the time has three <u>major</u> chords, even sometimes all three of them as dominant seven chords, and we still feel that a <u>minor</u> pentatonic scale sounds *really good* over all three of them. We are used to it, we have heard it and played it like that thousands of times... so many times in fact, that it is a very "bluesy" thing to hear and play.

That, ladies and gentlemen, is the power of "cultural weight".

Rhythm Changes
simple scale study in C

Sergio R. Klein

Rhythm Changes

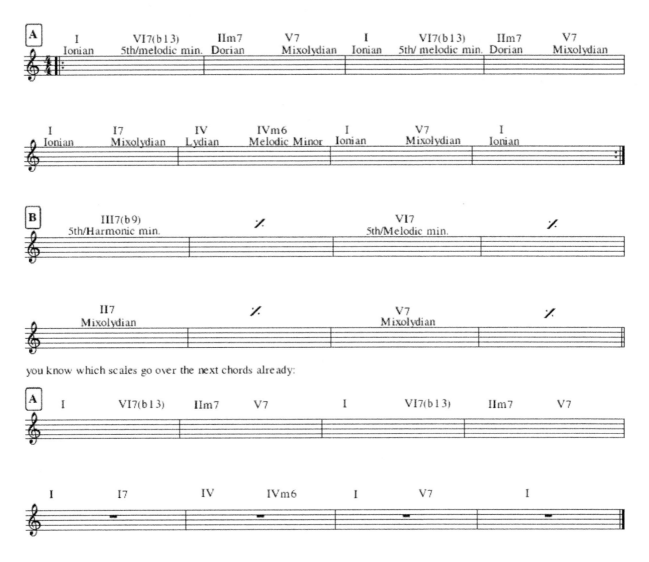

you know which scales go over the next chords already:

Ionian: 1 2 3 4 5 6 7

5th mode melodic minor: 1 2 3 4 5 b6 b7

Dorian: 1 2 b3 4 5 6 b7

Mixolydian: 1 2 3 4 5 6 b7

Lydian: 1 2 3 #4 5 6 7

Melodic Minor: 1 2 b3 4 5 6 7

5th mode harmonic minor: 1 b2 3 4 5 b6 b7

Turnarounds

Turnaround Basics

At the end of many jazz, pop and blues tunes, there are often two bars of the tonic chord (I). It is very common for good performers and composers/arrangers to substitute these two bars for a **"turnaround"**, this helps the harmonic motion or "harmonic rhythm" of the song to keep moving forward.

Some really good performers will often perform a different turnaround every time they play through the form.

The simplest way to "solve" the "problem" of having two bars with the same chord at the end of a tune (after a couple of play-troughs it can start to sound too repetitive), would be to play a V7 for the duration of the last bar (ex.1) or just for the second half of it (ex.2):

Ex.1

Ex.2

Another often used turnaround is to insert a II-V-I into the last two bars:

Ex.3

Yet another method to make those last two bars more interesting is to insert a
VI-II-V-I progression in the last bar (Ex.5) or to spread it out over the last two bars (Ex.6).

Ex.5

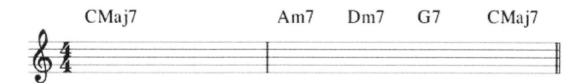

Ex.6

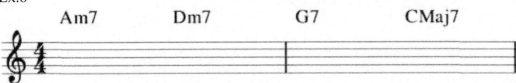

This is a VIm7 IIm7 V7 IMaj7 progression. It is not a turnaround *per sé*, but it is used quite often at the end of a tune to "go back" to the beginning... and that's what a turnaround is, so I opted to include it here also.

There are a lot of variations of this progression and also of the II-V-I alone. This is why I opted to dedicate a whole chapter to each of those cases separately.

It is really helpful for beginning improvisers to learn how to play over standard turnarounds, obviously transposing them into all 12 keys.

What I did when I was learning them, was transcribe what my favourite players were playing over turnarounds, and then practice those phrases in all 12 keys. Then I started to create variations of those phrases until they became something different, something that was my own.

This also develops your ear quite a bit – your ears and finger will be flying over those changes in no time.

The following pages are a list of the most commonly used variations of turnarounds you will find.

I am also adding practice variations for each example.

I want you to transpose every example I give you and apply them then to each variation on the list.

Now let's get started.

Most Common Turnaround Variations List
and Some Practice Ideas

1) <u>V7 in the second bar</u>:

To start practicing ANY progression you learn from now on, I want to recommend this method to you. It is both the simplest one and the one that teaches your ears the "whole sound" of the chord by playing the correspondent scale over it.

Just play the mode for each chord ascending starting from the root. If you play eighth notes in a 4/4 bar, you will get a whole octave.

Over the IMaj7 chord, we use the Ionian Mode (Major Scale).

Formula: 1   2   3   4   5   6   7   chord tensions: 9   13

Over the V7 chord, we play the Mixolydian Mode.

Formula: 1   2   3   4   5   6   b7   chord tensions: 9   13

2) <u>IIm7 - V7</u> in the second bar:

To keep the "starting on the root" idea, practice like this at first:

Ascend using the Major Scale over the IMaj7 chord using eighth notes. In measure 2, start at the root of the IIm7 chord and descend. Also, use eighth notes so you land on the root of the V7 chord.

Over IIm7 we play the Dorian mode.

Formula: 1   2   b3   4   5   6   b7   chord tensions: 9   11   13

You MUST use some sort of backing track, or else it will just sound like you are playing up and down on the Major Scale. In fact, you must ALWAYS use a backing track.

The absence of a repetition symbol at the end of each example is just to remind you to transpose it into the other 11 keys...when you are done with each one of those, you are allowed to start from bar one again.

3) <u>IMaj7 - VIm7 in the first bar; IIm7 - G7 in the second bar:</u>

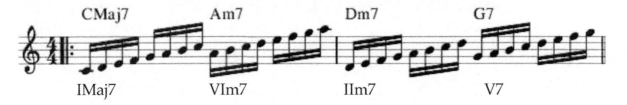

Over VIm7 we play Aeolian mode.

Formula: 1 2 b3 4 5 b6 b7   chord tensions: 9 11

This is a good way to practice your scales. In order to get a full octave, we play sixteenth notes now.

4) <u>IMaj7 - VI7 in the first bar; IIm7 - V7 in the second bar:</u>

This is a small variation from the previous example. Instead of playing VIm7 on the first bar, we play VI7. This chord is the secondary dominant of IIm7. Remember: secondary dominants are dominant chords with a diatonic root, and that resolve a 4th up or a 5th down into a chord different from the root. They have at least one non-diatonic note.

The secondary dominant of IIm7, VI7, uses the 5th mode of the Melodic Minor Scale, also known as Mixolydian b6.

Formula: 1 2 3 4 5 b6 b7   tensions: 9 b13

Another way to practice scales is to play them descending starting and ending on the root. Simple and effective.

5) <u>IIIm7 - VIm7 in the first bar; IIm7 and V7 in the second bar:</u>

There is no non-diatonic chord in this variation. We just substitute the IMaj7 for a IIIm7 in the first bar.

Where the whole octave scales practice idea was going is now quite obvious: Start at the root and ascend on one chord, start at the root of the next chord and descend.

We will take a look at other things you can do to practice scales, don't worry. Important for now is that you realize that ALL the scale practice exercises you already know can and should be applied to every chord progression you learn. In every key of course.

Doing that will save you a LOT of time.

Not only will you be practicing your scales, but you will be practicing them in a <u>musical context</u>, how they relate to each other and how that relationship <u>sounds</u> at the same time. Furthermore, you will be learning all of these really useful and common chord progressions and how harmony actually works.

Ok let's continue with the turnaround variations.

6) <u>III7 and VI7 in the first bar; II7 and V7 in the second bar</u>:

This is very common. III7 is the secondary dominant of VIm7. In this progression however, VI is present as VI7, which is the secondary dominant of IIm7. II in this progression is played as II7, which is the secondary dominant of V7!

This series of dominant chords, which should resolve into a diatonic chord, but instead resolve a 4th up or down a 5th into another secondary dominant, is called an "extended dominant" series.

The root into which each chord resolves is the one we expect; the quality of the chord is dominant 7th. In other words: we "extend" the dominant <u>function</u> throughout the entire progression. We don't resolve that tension until we reach the IMaj7, normally found at the beginning of the tune.

Although some could argue that you can use the Mixolydian Mode on each chord, there are better options in my opinion. They sound more interesting and actually help to outline the overall key in which we are playing more effectively.

This practice example idea is really simple, but important to practice. We connect the scales by starting the next one at the nearest common note. This can teach you melodic fluidity while modulating. It is more often heard in modern "rock fusion" style guitar players like Guthrie Govan, Ritchie Kotzen, Greg Howe and Tom Quayle, to name a few.

Over III7 play the 5th mode of Harmonic Minor.

Formula: 1 b2 3 4 5 b6 b7   chord tensions: b9 b13

Over VI7 play the 5th mode of Melodic Minor.

Formula: 1 2 3 4 5 b6 b7   chord tensions: 9 b13

Over II7 and V7 play the Mixolydian Mode.

Formula: 1 2 3 4 5 6 b7   chord tensions: 9 13
7) <u>IIIm7 - bIII7 in the first bar; IIm7 - bII7 in the second bar.</u>

The scale practice example here targets one of the Guide Tones of the chord in which we resolve, in this case, the 3rd of the chord.

We start on the root of the first chord (if you practice on all 12 keys, this will be the only chord where you start on the root, all subsequent IIIm7 chords will start on the 3rd), we ascend through the scale and then we connect the scales by starting the next one at the 3rd.

We have two non-diatonic chords here: bIII7 and bII7. This variation is considered one of many variations for the I - VI - II - V progression. I explain this progression in detail in the chapter "The I-VI-II-V-I Progression".

I included it in this chapter nonetheless, because it is also a very common turnaround.

If you feel you still aren't prepared to practice it and would rather focus on the ones you think you can handle better for now, it is perfectly okay. Eventually you will learn them all anyway. It is not a rush to the top – that doesn't really exist in art. Just constant, steady hard work.

As I said; further in this book you will learn the "ins and outs".

For now, I just want you to memorize and start practicing the scales we use when facing these chord changes. As my teacher used to say, *"Get it into your ears and fingers first, then into your head. It's way easier this way and you will save time. Everything you learn with your brain after getting it into your ears, will feel easier... obvious even"*

So here we go:

Over IIIm7 play the Phrygian Mode; always.

Formula: 1   b2   b3   4   5   b6   b7   chord tensions: 11

By the way: if you think I repeat the formulas too much, it is on purpose. I REALLY want you to memorize them, even at the risk of annoying you. It is THAT important.

Over bIII7, the tritone substitution of VI7, play the glorious Lydian Dominant Mode, the 4th mode of the Melodic Minor Scale.

Formula: 1   2   3   #4   5   6   b7   chord tensions: 9   #11   13

As a rule, every non-diatonic dominant seventh chord resolving a half-step down or a whole-step up uses the Lydian Dominant Mode.
If you are really dying to know why right now, I explain it in fairly good detail in the "I-VI-II-V-I" chapter, 10th progression variation.

The first chord in the last bar in this turnaround is a IIm7, which, as you know, *screams* Dorian Mode. So that's what we always play over IIm7. Forever. Until the end of time... Dooooorian... dorian...

Formula, surely annoying by now: 1   2   b3   4   5   6   b7   tensions: 9   11   13

The last chord is bII7, the tritone substitution of V7. This one also resolves a half-step down to I when we go back to the top of the tune, so we use the Lydian Dominant Mode here too.

And no, I won't write the formula again, I mean: it is just up there! Look 16 lines up.

8) The "Lazy Bird" turnaround: IMaj7 - bIIIMaj7 - bVIMaj7 - bIIMaj7

Named after "Lazy Bird", a famous jazz standard by the great John Coltrane. This turnaround is very often used on the last two bars of that tune.

All of these chords are Maj7 chords, so the best choice really is the Lydian Mode. Not to mention, there is a "rule" which says that over non-diatonic Maj7 chords the scale of choice is the Lydian Mode. The major scale/Ionian Mode can work as well, it is just not "great".

There is ONE thing, though, that's pretty amazing. I mean: REALLY AMAZING.

I used this practice method to write the example above.

For the first chord, the IMaj7 uses Lydian mode; no surprise there, BUT on EVERY other chord, you can play a minor pentatonic scale whose root is the same as the IMaj7 chord in bar 1 (let's call this I Minor Pentatonic). This means that in the key of C Major, you can play C Minor Pentatonic over EbMaj7, AbMaj7 and DbMaj7!

Why does this work? And not only that, why it is so desirable to do so?

Ok look, the C Minor Pentatonic is C Eb F G Bb.
$$1 \quad b3 \quad 4 \quad 5 \quad b7 = \text{Minor Pentatonic formula btw.}$$

Now let's see what that means for each chord in this progression.

On EbMaj7   C is the 13th...check!
                  Eb is the root...check!
                  F is the 9th...check!
                  G is the 3rd...check!
                  Bb is the 5th...check!

So the C Minor Pentatonic Scale includes one guide tone, the 3rd and two chord tensions, the 9th and the 13th. You also get the root and the 5th.

This is actually also the Eb Major Pentatonic: Eb F G Bb C
                                            1 9 3 5 6
But for now, let's just think of it as C Minor Pentatonic... less things in your head.

On AbMaj7   C is the 3rd...check!
                  Eb is the 5th...check!
                  F is the 13th...check!
                  G is of course the major 7th...check!
                  Bb is the 9th...check!

Again, we get the 3rd, a guide tone, the 5th, the 13th (another tension), the major 7th (the other guide tone – awesome!) and the 9th!

On DbMaj7   C is the major 7th, guide tone, cool... yes please!
                    Eb is the 9th, tension, alright!
                    F is the 3rd, another guide tone... keep 'em coming
                    G is the coolest tension in the universe, the #11th
                    Bb is the 13th... yeah baby!

I mean, come on!

- It's easy to remember
- It sounds bluesy
- It sounds very modern, because we are accentuating tensions on all of the chords, not to mention all tensions – 9, #11 and 13 – on the last chord
- We are outlining the harmony perfectly if we start on every chord with a guide tone and,
- It is easier to keep melodic consistency due to the fact that we just have to think about ONE scale, freeing processing space for everything else... I just love it.

9) <u>IMaj7 - bIII7 - bVIMaj7 - bII7</u>

This one starts with IMaj7, so we use the major scale over this chord. You can definitely play Lydian if you prefer though. It is up to you.

Then we have bIII7, the tritone substitution of VI7. We use the Lydian Dominant Mode over this chord.

Instead of resolving a half step down into a IIm7, bIII7 resolves a 4th up into a non-diatonic bVIMaj7. Here we have a couple of options.

1. Play the Lydian Mode. This mode fits every non-diatonic Maj7 chord you will encounter, so I encourage you to practice this scale over this chord first.

2. Play I Minor Pentatonic. As we saw in example 8) above, playing the I minor pentatonic over bVIMaj7 is the same as playing both guide tones – the 3rd and the 7th – plus two tensions – the 9th and 13th and the 5th.

In this case, though, the next chord is a bII7, so the Minor Pentatonic of I doesn't fit, as its root is the major 7th of the bII chord. You could still play it as a chromatic neighbor tone or just completely avoid it and play the rest of the notes, ignoring the root.

I still have to mention it, because you might play a wonderful phrase based on I Minor Pentatonic over the bVIMaj7 chord and not want to interrupt it when reaching the next chord. If this happens, just ignore the root. Phrasing and melodic consistency are always preferable over "harmony on paper".

After bVIMaj7 we have bII7, the tritone substitution of V7. As you know by now, the scale that fits this chord is Lydian Dominant.
In the example I wrote for you to practice this variation, you will notice that I used arpeggios instead of scales. In this case, 7th chord arpeggios.
The idea is pretty simple: start one arpeggio in the direction you choose, ascending or descending, and connect to the next arpeggio at any note and play it in the opposite direction.

10) IMaj7 - #Idim7 - IIm7 - V7

Scale-wise, what we play over IMaj7, IIm7 and V7 is what we have been playing so far over them, nothing new: Ionian or Lydian over IMaj7, Dorian over IIm7 and Mixolydian over V7.

Now, over #Idim7 we play the 7th mode of the Harmonic Minor Scale, or if you prefer, II Harmonic Minor. (Why II Harmonic Minor? Because the scale based off the root of the 7th mode of Harmonic Minor contains the same notes as those in the Hrmonic Minor Scale based on the root of the II chord in this key. Got it? Good.)

7th mode of Harmonic Minor formula: 1   2   3   b4   b5   b6   bb7

On a side note: instead of writing "bb7" for the diminished 7th, we ca just write "6", as it is exactly the same pitch. It is 100% "official" too. I mention it because you will encounter one or the other in different contexts. Both refer to the same note.

Nowadays many musicians also play the "half-step/whole-step" diminished scale over this chord.

There are many ways to approach this chord, for example: to play a IVMaj7#5 chord or just an augmented triad (this is the arpeggio of the 3rd mode of Harmonic Minor), but for now let's keep it as simple as possible by playing the 7th mode of harmonic minor with the root on the #I.

As I mentioned before, you can think "Harmonic Minor Scale with root on II", just make sure that the notes you accentuate are the guide tones of #Idim7.

The arpeggio approach is quite simple and effective. Just practice the corresponding arpeggios for each chord and connect them.

In the example above, I started the first chord on a guide tone, the 3rd, the second chord on its root, the IIm7 on its 3rd and the last chord on its 7th, also a guide tone.

I did this in order to remind you that you can, and should, practice your arpeggios starting on each of its notes, preferably one of the guide tones (1st and 3rd chord inversion).

11) IMaj7 - bIIIdim7 - IIm7 - bII7

We have already covered three of these chords before: IMaj7, IIm7 and bII7. Just play the same scales you have been practicing over them up until now.

The new kid here is the bIIIdim7. Over this chord we also play the 7th mode of Harmonic Minor.

Remember its formula: 1   2   3   b4   b5   b6   bb7

In the practice example for this turnaround, I used a "1 2 3 5" pattern.
As you know, "1 2 3 5" refers to the degrees of the scale, not the specific quality of the interval, so if the scale has a minor 3rd instead of a major one, we just play the minor 3rd where the "3" in the pattern appears.

The same goes for every degree of the scale.

12) IMaj7 - VI7 - bVI7 - V7

This turnaround sounds very interesting. You already know what to use over the first chord and the last chord, so let's concentrate on the VI7 and bVI7 chords.

Over VI7, the secondary dominant of IIm7, we use the 5th mode of Melodic Minor. This chord usually anticipates a resolution into a IIm chord. In this case though, it does not. Instead we have another dominant chord a half step down: bVI7.

This "deception" doesn't sound "shocking" at all, due to two things:

1. The root movement is chromatic. This pleases our "western-educated" ears.

2. Each note of VI7 is a chromatic approach to a note from bVI7, as both chords have the same quality.

Overall this chord change sounds really good.

Over bVI7, the tritone substitution of II7, we play the 4th mode of Melodic Minor: Lydian Dominant.

In the practice example, I wrote a very common method of practicing scales. We chose one interval, in this case the 4th, and we play that interval up from every note throughout the whole progression.

If your instrument doesn't cover enough octaves, just change the octave at some point and continue playing the interval pattern.

Of course you can choose any interval you want, whenever you want. Important is that you eventually practice them all.

What I found interesting about this turnaround in particular when learning it for the first time was that you don't play the same dominant scale over all its dominant 7th chords.

You have Mixolydian b6 for the VI7, Lydian Dominant for the bVI7 and Mixolydian for the V7.

That makes this a great turnaround for scale practice.

It is worth noting that many players do, in fact, play Lydian Dominant over all three chords.

Remember: dominant 7th chords can take a lot of punishment. Many scales will sound terrific over them.

Every dominant scale (scales with a major 3rd and minor 7th, including some symmetric scales), no matter how many alterations and tensions it has, can be played over a dominant chord.

You surely will need and want to practice these other scales over your dominant 7th chords, and I really hope you do. But I cannot stress enough how important it is for you to learn and master the scale choices I am giving to you in this book first.

The knowledge you are acquiring right now will be the foundation upon which you will build your own harmonic language in the future.

13) <u>IMaj7 - VI7 - bV7 - bIII7</u>

This one is really interesting. Its root movement is based on a symmetric subdivision of the octave: we divide it in four equal parts, which gives us four minor 3rds.

In this turnaround, we use each of the resulting notes as a root for each chord.

This results in a minor 3rd descending root movement. After playing the fourth chord, we move a minor third down again and come back to the first chord, giving the feeling of resolution.

This is why it is also known as the "minor third cycle". No matter on which note you start the sequence, if you keep moving from minor 3rd to minor 3rd, you will always come back to the first note.

There are three possible minor thirds cycles:

1. C - A - Gb (F#) - Eb

2. D - B - Ab (G#) - F

3. Db - Bb - G - E

This simplifies the study of this turnaround, because you just need to practice these three cycles in order to cover every key.

Before I explain to you why this progression works and also why it is so interesting, let me first tell you about what to play over these chords and the practice idea I wrote for you on this example.

IMaj7 = Major Scale or Lydian Mode (maybe you had doubts, who knows?)

VI7 = 5th mode of Melodic Minor (Mixolydian b6)

bV7 and bIII7 = Lydian Dominant

The melodic idea I chose for this example is quite simple:

Play the 1 2 3 5 digital pattern on the first beat of each chord and on the second beat, play a descending arpeggio starting on the root all the way down to the 3rd.

So far, so good.

Now let me tell you a couple of things about the symmetric subdivisions of the octave to help you understand where these ideas come from.

Our western music is by and large based on an asymmetrical division of the octave: the Major Scale, Harmonic Minor Scale, Melodic Minor Scale and chords are all build stacking different qualities of thirds.

There are other ways to subdivide the octave that are purely mathematical.
We take the number of half-steps an octave has, twelve, and we divide it in equal parts.

We can obviously divide an octave in twelve equal parts, 12 semitones, and we get the chromatic scale. This doesn't give us anything new to play with so we will focus on all the other symmetric subdivisions we can get out of it.

Let's take a look at an octave starting on the note C:

- We can divide it in two equal parts, 6 half-steps each, and we get two tritones:

C - F# and F# - C

- We can divide it in three equal parts, 4 half-steps each, and we get 3 major 3rds:

C - E   E - G#   G# - C (B#)

- When we divide it in four equal parts, we get <u>four minor 3rds</u>:

C - Eb   Eb - Gb   Gb - A (Bbb)   A - C

- If divided in six equal parts, we get <u>six major 2nds</u>:

C - D; D - E; E - F#; F# - G#; G# - A#; A# - C

If you take a closer look, you will notice that the 3 notes we get by dividing the octave in three equal parts form an augmented triad; the 4 notes from dividing the octave by four equal parts form a dim7 chord and the 6-part equal division gives us a whole-tone scale, also known as the Hexatonic Scale (Hexa= six).

This opens up a lot of possibilities, both melodic and harmonic.

In this turnaround, the notes we get from dividing the octave in four minor 3rds are used as roots for each chord. This keeps adding tension to the progression until we finally resolve it by coming back to the I chord at the top of the tune.

Our brain recognizes the pattern and the resolution feels pleasant. It "makes sense" by the time we reach the I chord again.

Repetition is a powerful tool indeed...

Historically speaking, the employment of symmetrical divisions of the octave is not as new as most musicians may think. It can be traced back to at least 1825, when the Austrian composer Franz Schubert based a series of modulations on them.

Wolf, Brahms, Rimsky-Korsakov, Scriabin and the great Stravinsky (and by "great" I mean GREAT) are some other composers who have explored the symmetric division of the octave.

With "Giant Steps", John Coltrane brought this harmonic concept into the awareness of jazz musicians and until this very day it serves as inspiration for many.

14) IMaj7 - VI7 - bVII7 - VII7

I don't really like this turnaround much, but you will encounter it more than a couple times, so it was necessary to include it.
No chord is new here, but the way they are presented is.

The first chord is IMaj7, nothing new going on there. Same chord, same scale as usual.

The second chord is the secondary dominant of II: VI7... nothing new, there either. Same scale over this chord also.

A half-tone above we have a bVII7... again, nothing different with this one either. bVII7 = Lydian Dominant Mode.

A half step above this chord, we have a VII7. 5th mode of Harmonic Minor goes over this one. Also nothing new.

These are the more "correct" scales you should learn over this turnaround, but you should know that a good number of players just play Lydian Dominant over all these chords.

If I were you, I would practice and master the more "correct" choice first, THEN I would start practicing whichever dominant scale I want over my dominant chords.

We live in amazing times to play music. As I've said before: dominant chords can take LOTS of punishment. If phrased right, you can get away with playing almost anything over a Dominant 7 chord.

You will notice this when you start to transcribe Michael Brecker, Pat Metheny, Allan Holdsworth, John Stowell, Scott Kinsey, etc.

The root motion in this turnaround is ascending and chromatic from the VI7 chord on.

Although this is a smooth root movement, it isn't quite as pleasant to the ear as the descending chromatic movement. The resolution doesn't feel as final.

It can be good if you want to achieve exactly that: not to sound as final.
For this reason, you may be better off using it at some point near the end of your play-throughs, just not at the very end.

For the melodic practice suggestion on this last turnaround example, I wanted to give you a less "pattern-ish" idea to practice, so I mixed a couple of previous ideas, plus an eight-note cell pattern we haven't use yet.

On the first beat of the first chord you play a descending arpeggio starting on the 3rd and without the root: 3 - 7 - 5 - 3.

On the second beat of the first chord you play that 1 2 3 5 digital pattern.

On the first beat of the second chord you start by playing a descending arpeggio from the root and ending on the 3rd: 1 - b7 - 5 - 3. On the last beat of that bar you play a 1 2 3 5 digital pattern again.
In the second bar you play an eight-note digital pattern or "note cell", if you prefer:

$$1 - 5 - 3 - 2 - 1 - 2 - 3 - 5$$

You do the same for the last chord.

Turnaround Formula 1 in all 12 Keys

Sergio Klein

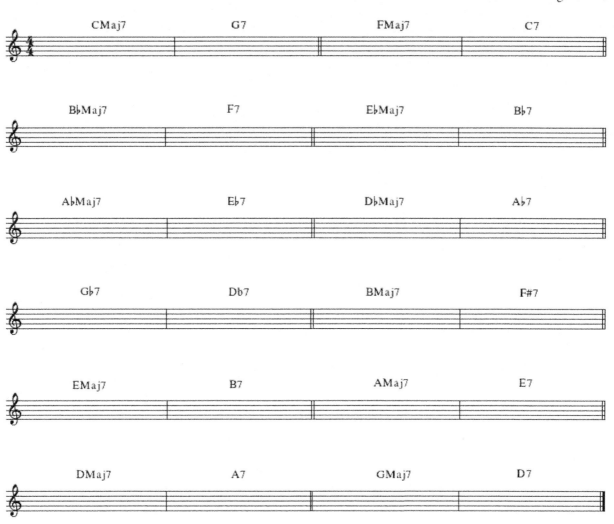

Turnaround Formula 2 in all 12 Keys

Sergio Klein

Turnaround Formula 3 in all 12 Keys

Sergio Klein

Turnaround Formula 4 in all 12 Keys

Sergio Klein

Turnaround Formula 5 in all 12 Keys

Sergio Klein

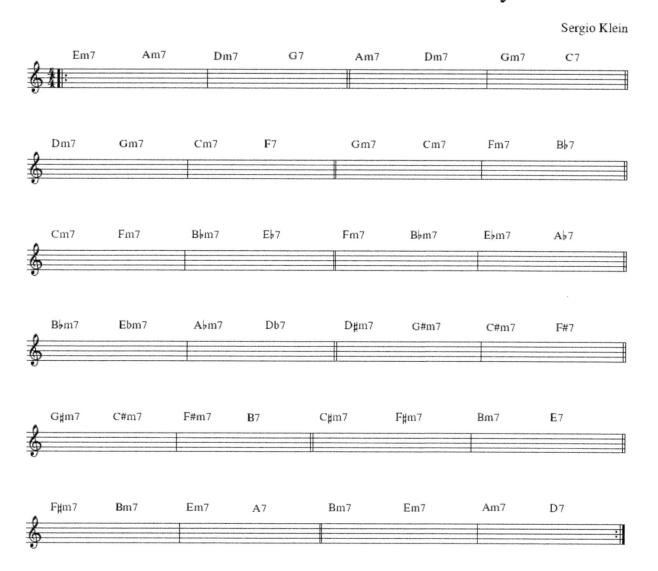

Turnaround Formula 6 in all 12 Keys

Sergio Klein

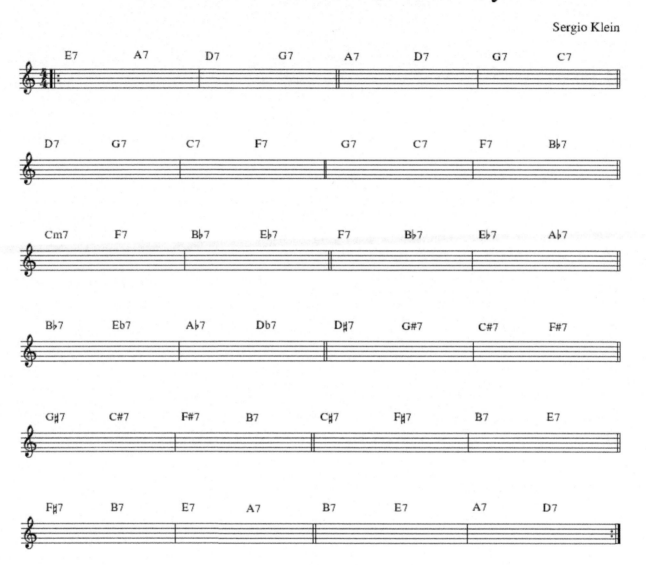

Turnaround Formula 7 in all 12 Keys

Sergio Klein

Turnaround Formula 8 in all 12 Keys

Sergio Klein

Turnaround Formula 9 in all 12 Keys

Sergio Klein

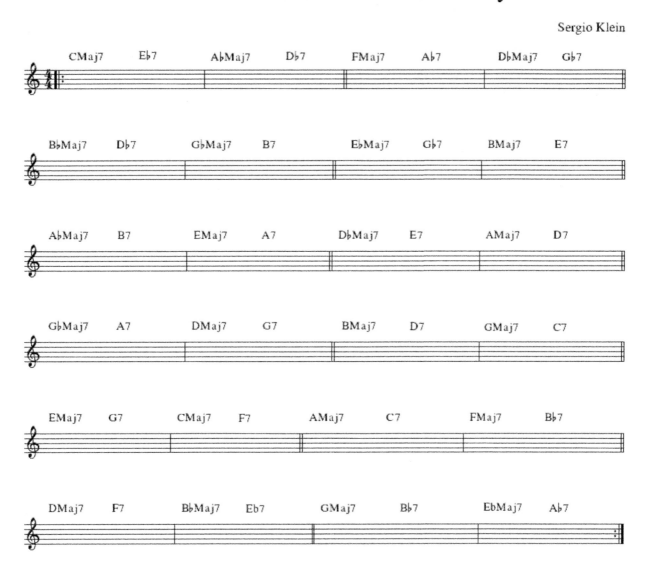

Turnaround Formula 10 in all 12 Keys

Sergio Klein

Turnaround Formula 11 in all 12 Keys

Sergio Klein

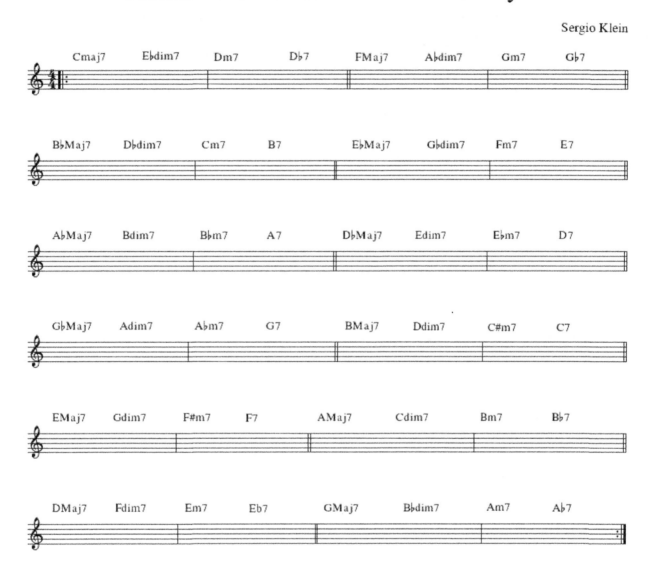

Turnaround Formula 12 in all 12 Keys

Sergio Klein

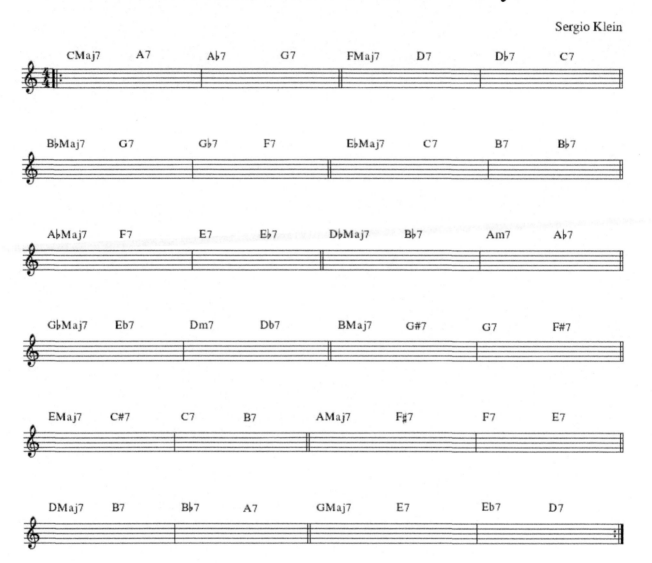

Turnaround Formula 13 in all 12 Keys

Sergio Klein

Turnaround Formula 14 in all 12 Keys

Sergio Klein

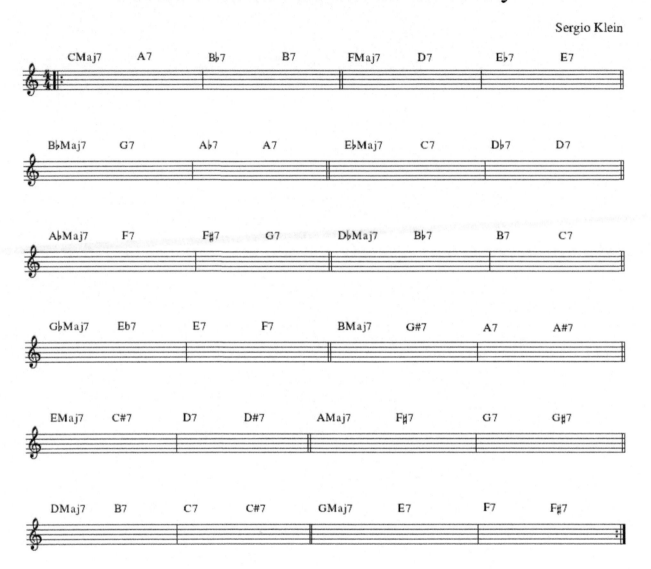

The I VI II V I Progression

The I-VI-II-V-I Progression

This progression is quite popular. It is often as heard in jazz, as well as in other kinds of music. Sometimes it is used at the end of a song (or form) as a turnaround, in some cases it becomes the very skeleton of a tune. The jazz standard "All The Things You Are" by Jerome Kern is a really good example of this progression (Oscar Hammerstein wrote the lyrics).

Most of the time, you will encounter this progression as **IMaj7-VIm7-IIm7-IMaj7** in the same key, meaning of course, that you can play the same scale over all of the four chords which constitute the progression. This certainly makes life easier for beginning improvisers.

To stay in the same key, use the Aeolian Mode on the VIm7 instead of Dorian.

It is very important, though, to be aware of the exact chord you are playing over and then use the chords to dictate your note choice. Even if you feel tempted to just run over the progression with just that one major scale, make sure the changes and the colour of each chord influence your improvisation. A good method for this is to start and resolve on one of the guide tones of each chord (3rd and 7th; 3rd and 7th, 3rd and 7th... let that be your mantra for a while).

There are many variations of this progression, most of them just replace one chord for another with the same harmonic function as the original chord. For example, replacing the I for the III of the same key. These chords have all their notes in common except for the root.

This leaves us with a IIIm7-VIm7-IIm7-V7-IMaj7.

Replacing the I for a III at the beginning of the progression gives us a cycle of 4ths root motion. This makes it easy for listeners to "predict" the next chord. You'll find this variation popping up a lot.

Another variation you will encounter, is the one which replaces the IIm7 for a II7 (secondary dominant of V), keeping the 4ths root motion and strongly anticipating the upcoming V7 at the same time. As you know, on II7 we play the Mixolydian Mode.

On the next page I wrote most of the I-VI-II-V-I variations you will encounter and also which scales apply to each chord.

I-VI-II-V-I Variations List

1)   IMaj7   VIm7   IIm7   V7   IMaj7

2)   IMaj7   VI7   IIm7   V7   IMaj7

3)   IMaj7   VI7   II7   V7   IMaj7

4)   IMaj7   bIII7   IIm7   bII7   IMaj7

5)   IMaj7   VI7   bVI7   V7   IMaj7

6)   IMaj7   #I°7   IIm7   #II°7   IIIm7

7)   IMaj7   #I°7   IIm7   II°7   IMaj7

8)   IIIm7   VIm7   IIm7   V7   IMaj7

9)   IIIm7   VIm7   II7   V7   IMaj7

10)   IIIm7   bIII7   IIm7   bII7   IMaj7

I am pretty sure that after learning all of the previous progressions, and all the theory behind them, you have a pretty good idea of what harmonic tools come into play in all of these I-VI-II-V-I variations.

Let's review these progressions one by one, so you can confirm the knowledge you have acquired so far. If I start to sound redundant to you, rejoice! You: have come a long way in understanding how our western harmonic system works. Me: I am achieving my goal of unlocking this information – you're learning!

Ok, enough rejoicing. We still have some work to do.

Scale Practice Guide

1) IMaj7   VIm7   IIm7   V7   IMaj7

This one doesn't need much explanation. Every chord is in the same key, so we play the corresponding mode for each chord, namely:

- Ionian or Lydian over IMaj7 (it is a matter of preference, but that juicy #11th... just saying...).

On a side note: Something I really like to do, though, is play Ionian over the first IMaj7 of the progression and then play Lydian over the last IMaj7, preferably having the #11th to be the last note of my phrase. It just kills.

- Aeolian over VIm7
- Dorian over IIm7
- Mixolydian over V7

Use these three scales for those chords on all variations. And that's it.

2) IMaj7   <u>VI7</u>   IIm7   V7   IMaj7

Now here, the only thing that is different is the VI7 chord, over which we play 5th mode of Melodic Minor (Mixolydian b6) : 1   2   3   4   5   b6   b7

You *could* use the 5th mode of Harmonic Minor, but in this case (VI7) you have to change less notes from the original key if you go for Mixolydian b6. If we were in the key of C, we would just have to change C into C# in order to get A Mixolydian b6.

A Mixolydian b6 = A B <u>C#</u> D E F G - it sounds really good; jazzier and smoother.

A Phrygian Dominant = A <u>Bb</u> <u>C#</u> D E F G - less desirable, but sounds good too.

3) IMaj7   VI7   <u>II7</u>   V7   IMaj7

In comparison to the previous one, the only thing which changes is the IIm7, which now is a II7. You know that over II7 we play the Mixolydian Mode, so that is what we are going to do.

Redundant memory helper: the Mixolydian Mode formula: 1   2   3   4   5   6   b7

We still play Mixolydian b6 or Phrygian Dominant over VI7, btw.

4) IMaj7   <u>bIII7</u>   IIm7   <u>bII7</u>   IMaj7

This progression is a variation of the previous one and I've got to tell you: I really like the smoothness of this one. It uses the tritone substitution of bIII7 for VI7 and the tritone substitution of bII7 for V7, to give the root movement that sweet descending chromatic movement. And not only that, the scale choice for both these chords is the Lydian Dominant Mode, one of my favourite modes of all time!

YES: ALL time!

The Lydian Dominant Mode's EPIC formula is: 1   2   3   #4   5   6   b7

5) IMaj7   VI7   <u>bVI7</u>   V7   IMaj7

In this one, bVI7 substitutes II7. Lydian Dominant is the scale to play here. As you know from the previous examples, VI7 uses 5th of Melodic Minor.

The chromatic descending root movement is always a nice touch and you find it here between the VI7, bVI7 and V7. Over IMaj7 and V7 we play the same scales we always have been – and you know which ones those are, right?

6) IMaj7   <u>#I°7</u>   IIm7   <u>#II°7</u>   IIIm7

Ok, this one is nice, it introduces two chords we haven't encountered before.
The #I°7 and the #II°7.

Why do they sound good? For a couple of reasons.

The most obvious reason is that they outline an ascending chromatic root movement between the chords. As you know by now, chromatics are really pleasant to our ears. The ascending movement also creates a feeling of "growing tension" that needs to resolve, thus giving the progression a strong sense of harmonic movement.

The other reason why these two diminished chords work is the following:

V7 chords can be also substituted by the VII° of a scale. They share almost every note, including that tritone which needs to resolve. You can see the VII° as a V7 played up from the third. In the C major scale:

G7= G   B   D   F

B°= B   D   F

B°7 = B   D   F   A – so we could analyze B°7 as G9 without the root.

Now, the °7 chord is also the 7th degree of the Harmonic Minor Scale. Because the chord into which these diminished chords resolves to in this progression ARE minor, that is the scale we are going to primarily use over those diminished chords: 7th mode of Harmonic Minor.
Some prefer to call it the "Ultralocrian Mode". That sounds like a "superhero" scale to me, so I just call it the "7th mode of Harmonic Minor". Call me "old school" if you want.

Formula time!   1   2   3   b4   b5   b6   bb7

Some prefer this way of writing the formula: 1   2   3   b4   b5   b6   **6**

Both are legit, so memorize the one that is easier for you.

The most common practice though (which I don't like that much to be completely honest) is to play just a diminished arpeggio. In my opinion, it messes with any melodic line you might have been developing up to that point.

For the IIIm7 chord use Phrygian Mode.

7) IMaj7   #I°7   IIm7   <u>II°7</u>   IMaj7

This is a variation of the previous progression, where instead of a #II°7 we have a II°7.
Now this chord also works, because the tritone formed by its 3rd and °7th is the same one formed by the 3rd and 7th of the V7. We don't call this tritone substitution though, because the quality of the chord changes.

I'll explain it in the key of C so its easier; the underlined fat notes form the tritone:

$$\textbf{V7} = G7 = G \ \underline{\textbf{B}} \ D \ \underline{\textbf{F}}$$

$$\textbf{bII7} = Db7 = Db \ \underline{\textbf{F}} \ Ab \ \underline{\textbf{Cb}} \ (B)$$

$$\textbf{II°7} = D \ \underline{\textbf{F}} \ Ab \ \underline{\textbf{Cb}}$$

This is why it works, the II°7 chord has a tritone which needs to resolve into the IMaj7.

Now in this case, the best scale choice in my opinion is the half-step/whole-step symmetric scale, also known as the "Eight Note Dominant Scale". As its name implies, it is constructed by alternating half-steps and whole-steps.

half step - whole step - half step - whole step - etc....

formula: 1 b2 #2 3 #4 5 6 b7

If you are playing over D°7 in the key of C, I recommend starting on a C note and then descending through the D Eight Note Dominant Scale to resolve into CMaj7. It sounds more resolutive.

Phrasing your way up is totally legit of course, but it can get pretty difficult for beginners to *not* make it sound "forced", if you know what I mean. Start by practicing it descending and once you have the sound of the scale in your ears, start making ascending phrases with it.

I really love this scale, it is totally worth the practice you'll put into it. Players like Allan Holdsworth and Wayne Krantz use it a lot. In good trained hands and ears, it can add a lot of sophistication to your playing.

8) <u>IIIm7</u>   VIm7   IIm7   V7   IMaj7

This is probably the variation you will encounter more often. As I told you at the beginning of this chapter, it produces a cycle of 4ths root motion between the chords, which helps the listener to "predict" the next chord.
When the "predicted" chord appears where expected = human brain happy = dopamine = success!

All the chords in this progression are diatonic. This means that you *can* play through it by just using the major scale of the key you are in. I encourage you, though, to outline the harmony by focusing on playing the corresponding mode for each chord.
It sounds overall more interesting, but it also trains an ability that's really useful when you have to play over chord changes in general. Not to mention that this kind of playing over changes is, more or less, a MUST for every jazz musician. It is deeply rooted in pretty much every jazz style since Miles and Trane.

Okay, so back to harmony:

The **IIIm7** substitutes the **IMaj7** at the beginning of the progression. By now you should know that these two chords share almost every note. You could look at it like this: Playing **IIIm7** is like playing **IMaj9** without the root.
To keep it diatonic, play:

Phrygian mode on the **IIIm7**
Aeolian mode on the **VIm7**
Dorian mode on the **IIm7**
Mixolydian on the **V7**
Ionian OR Lydian mode on the **IMaj7**

I know you know the formulas for these modes, so let's move on.

9) **IIIm7**   **VIm7**   **II7**   **V7**   **IMaj7**

A variation of the previous progression. Now, instead of the IIm7 appearing as the third chord, we have a IIm7. This is the secondary dominant of V7. In other words, it is the "dominant of the dominant". You just call it II7 and everyone will know what you are talking about.

II7 uses the Mixolydian Mode.

Use the corresponding modes for the other chords and *Voilà*! You have learned another REALLY common variation of the I - VI - II - V - I progression

10) **IIIm7**   **bIII7**   **IIm7**   **bII7**   **IMaj7**

Ok, if you compare this one with **IMaj7 bIII7 IIm7 bII7 IMaj7** (variation number 4, above), the only difference is that the first chord is substituted by the IIIm7, and as you know, this chord has the same harmonic function of IMaj7: tonic.

By substituting IMaj7 with IIIm7, we get an even smoother overall sound, due to the chromatic descending root motion throughout the whole progression.

Use the same modes as in the variation number 4 on the list, but play Phrygian on the IIIm7.

To sum everything up in the most practical way, here's the list of every scale you will need in order to practice these variations. I have classified them into diatonic and non-diatonic scales to make it easier for you. The diatonic scales have all of their notes in the overall key of the progression. The non-diatonic scales have at least one non-diatonic note.

Diatonic Modes:

Chord	Mode
IMaj7	Ionian: 1 2 3 4 5 6 7
IIm7	Dorian: 1 2 b3 4 5 6 b7
IIIm7	Phrygian: 1 b2 b3 4 5 b6 b7
V7	Mixolydian: 1 2 3 4 5 6 b7
VIm7	Aeolian: 1 2 b3 4 5 b6 b7

Non-Diatonic Modes:

Chords	Mode
II7	Mixolydian
bII7, bIII7 and bVI7	Lydian Dominant: 1 2 3 #4 5 6 b7
#II°7 and #I°7	7th Mode of Harmonic Minor: 1 2 3 b4 b5 b6 6
VI7	5th Mode of Melodic Minor: 1 2 3 4 5 b6 b7
II°7	Half Step/Whole-Step Scale: 1 b2 #2 3 #4 5 6 b7
IMaj7	Lydian Mode: 1 2 3 #4 5 6 7

I have underlined just the notes you should memorize, the specific combination of alterations to the major scale (1 2 3 4 5 6 7) which make each scale unique. It is easier to memorize them this way and at the same time it makes you more conscious of these very important notes.

I must mention that there is still another variation, the "Trane Variation", discovered by John Coltrane (one of my greatest heroes). It is also known as "Coltrane Changes".
In my opinion, one can fill a book of its own and you will encounter it literally in two songs: "Giant Steps" and "Countdown". And on "Countdown", what we encounter is a variation of the "original" Coltrane Changes found in "Giant Steps".

It is brilliant and sounds awesome in my opinion. It also became really important for the development of modern harmony, but for now let's reserve that topic for more advanced players (and another book).

Probably by now, you have been doing what I think almost everybody does while practicing scales: playing them up and down, applying patterns, playing arpeggios up, down, backwards, intervals, etc... ALL of this is very, VERY useful and you should keep doing it. But, and it is a BIG BUT (no pun intended), you can start doing all of this while practicing your progressions, too.
As a matter of fact, I rarely practice isolated scales anymore.

I just choose a progression which has the scale I want to practice, record a backing track for it (sometimes you get bored of playing over the same backing tracks every time) and then – slowly at first – practice my scales. First just in one key, maybe for 10 to 20 minutes, and then in ALL KEYS for an hour or so.

I concentrate on one specific thing at first. Let's look at an example. Let's say I want to practice my phrasing in Lydian Dominant.

The first thing I would do, would be to choose a progression which contains a chord over which I can play that scale:

IIIm7   bIII7   IIm7   bII7   IMaj7

That is Variation 10 on our list. This is a smart one to choose, because:

1 - I love it

2 - It contains two chords where the scale of choice is the Lydian dominant I'm so eager to practice.

To start practicing I would then record myself playing the chords. If you have a lazy day, then you can just go online and look for a suitable backing track, or even use your phone to record it and then connect your speakers to its headphone output. A good thing about recording them yourself is that you get the progression into your ears very quickly. In a couple of weeks of doing this, your ears will have already memorized a lot of progressions.

Then I would do one or two of the scale exercises I've been recommending you to do in the other units of this guide. By now you must have a couple of your own, too.

Then maybe you can get more specific, like: "I will play only 4ths intervals on my Lydian Dominant". I run through the progression, play whatever I decided on the other chords, but when I reach the bIII7, I only play in 4ths. Then I start on one of the guide tones of IIm7, then again play only 4ths on the bII7 and resolve to the IMaj7.
This is just one example.

There is NO REASON not to practice multiple things at the same time. In this case, we have practiced a scale we felt we should practice more, a progression which gives CONTEXT to the scale we want to practice and at the same time, we're forcing ourselves to tie a specific performance strategy (those 4th intervals) into our melodies.

It is a win-win-win-win situation which gives you the most results for the time invested.

So NO MORE "WATCHING TV" SCALE PRACTICE FOR YOU!!

I VI II V I Variations

scale usage

Sergio R. Klein

A

IMaj7	VIm7	IIm7	V7	IMaj7
Ionian	Aeolian	Dorian	Mixolydian	Ionian or lydian

B

IMaj7	VI7(b13)	IIm7	V7	IMaj7
Ionian	5th of melodic minor	Dorian	Mixolydian	Ionian or Lydian

C

IMaj7	VI7(b13)	II7	V7	IMaj7
Ionian	5th of melodic minor	Mixolydian	Mixolydian	Ionian or Lydian

D

IMaj7	bIII7	IIm7	bII7	IMaj7
Ionian	Lydian Dominant	Dorian	Lydian Dominant	Ionian or Lydian

E

IMaj7	VI7(b13)	bVI7	V7	IMaj7
Ionian	5th of Melodic Minor	Lydian Dominant	Mixolydian	Ionian or Lydian

F

IMaj7	#I°7	IIm7	#II°7	IIIm7
Ionian	7th of Harmonic Minor	Dorian	7th of Harmonic Minor	Phrygian

G

IMaj7	#I°7	IIm7	II°7	IMaj7
Ionian	7th of Harmonic Minor	Dorian	"eight note dominant scale"	Ionian or Lydian
			("half-step/whole-step scale")	

H

IIIm7	VIm7	IIm7	V7	IMaj7
Phrygian	Aeolian	Dorian	Mixolydian	Ionian or Lydian

I

IIIm7	VIm7	II7	V7	IMaj7
Phrygian	Aeolian	Mixolydian	Mixolydian	Ionian or Lydian

J

IIIm7	bIII7	IIm7	bII7	IMaj7
Phrygian	Lydian Dominant	Dorian	Lydian Dominant	Ionian or Lydian

I VI II V I - Variations

Exercises in C - Multiple Concepts

Sergio R. Klein

The Blues

The Blues Progression

How many times a day do we listen to any kind of music only to find ourselves discovering some sort of Blues influence in it? Sometimes it is the form, others a bit of articulation here and there, and sometimes it is a Blues Progression disguised as Funk, Electro, Fusion or another kind of music we don't immediately associate with the Blues.

For the general public, Blues can be many things: a certain "mood", a particular music style, a certain repertoire and so on.

For us musicians, the Blues is a musical FORM which can appear in any tempo, band configuration, feel, time signature, style and genre you can imagine.

There are two general statements we can make about Blues:

1 - Usually the length of a Blues form is 12 bars.

2 - It is based on three chords: the I, IV and V of a key

If you cover those two points and add a full orchestra, put a dog choir on top of it and play it underwater, a musician would still call it a blues.

The basic Blues progression looks like this:

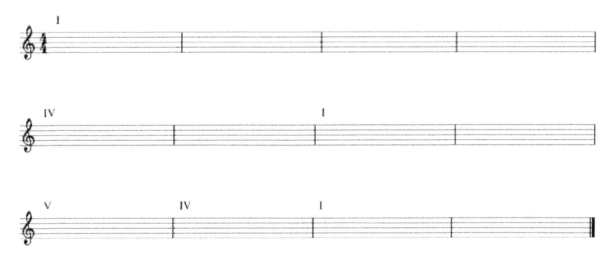

Every blues progression you will encounter is based upon this rather simple, but powerful harmonic scheme.

Four bars of the tonic (first degree or "I" from a key – not the drink), followed by two bars of the subdominant in the same key, then two more of the tonic. The last four bars are: one of the dominant followed by one measure of the subdominant and two of the tonic.

Why is it important to learn the form by its harmonic functions and not just simply as specific chords or tonal degrees?

Because this is THE thing that stays the same – the overall harmonic function of the Blues form.

This way you can also play a Minor Blues. It's just about keeping the tonal functions, but relating them to a minor key.

Just replace the I for a Im, the IV for a IVm and the V7 Mixolydian for a V7(b9) and *voilà!*: you have a Minor Blues.

We can use any chord substitution we want, a turnaround on the two last bars, II V I, etc. This makes the harmony _sound_ different, but it leaves the tonal functions unaltered.

Employing chord substitutions, inserting chords and cadences, _without altering the harmonic function_ of each measure, are common practices musicians employ to give the Blues progression more variety and texture.

In other words: We cannot change the overall harmonic structure of a Blues, just its character or color. If we change the overall harmonic structure, we can no longer call it a Blues.

A very common way to create variations of the Blues progression is to play the I and the IV as Dominant 7th chords. Having, potentially, four different dominant seven chords, the Blues opens up many harmonic opportunities. Just think about how many dominant scales are out there... you can imagine how rich and challenging a Blues can become at its full potential!

This is one more reason why so many contemporary players haven't left the Blues in the past. It is a really nice way to combine modern harmony with a musical form that is well known by musicians and non-musicians alike. Keep this in mind when practicing the Blues.

Here are a couple of common Blues Progressions for you to practice.

Notice that sometimes, as in the first progression, I've written the I and IV as Dominant 7 chords. I have done this because this is the most common way to play those chords in jam sessions.

Also common is to play the I chord as a I6 chord.

I've added some examples of Blues progression variations, which use some more complex substitutions and cadences: the "Parker Blues" or "Bird Blues" and a couple of typical Jazz Blues progressions.

Before you start practicing those two, I recommend that you read the "The Right Scale" scale/chord relationship summary and then go through the "II V I", "VI II V I "and "Turnaround" chapters of this book.

In those chapters, you will find all the information you need to fully understand the Parker Blues and Jazz Blues progressions.

There is no hurry though. Remember: learning music and how to make art is a _process_, *not* a race.

Be a good artist... leave the racing to the athletes.

Blues Progression Examples

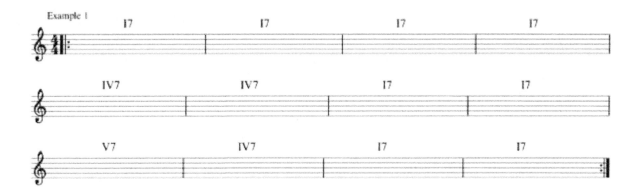

This is perhaps the first Blues you learned. It is just the very basic Blues progression, but every chord is played as a tetrad. A Dominant 7 chord to be more precise.

You can play a Minor Pentatonic/Blues Scale with root on the "I" throughout the whole progression. You can also play the Mixolydian Mode on any of these chords.

To add more flavor, you can also try out different dominant scales over any chord, like the Lydian Dominant Mode or even the Altered Scale. To keep it "bluesy" though, you should try to resolve into the blues scale from time to time.
Are you starting to see the potential of this form? It seems really simple at first glance, but offers so many possibilities... it becomes really addictive.

Listen to any one of the best contemporary jazz/blues/fusion musicians of any era and you will find they use this approach all the time.

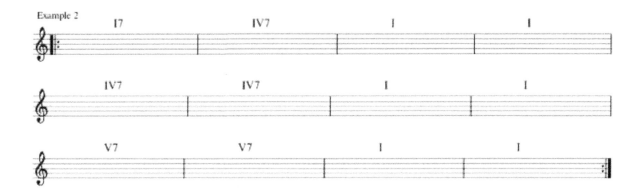

The only thing that really changes in this variation is the **IV7** chord in the second bar. I wrote the **I** chord as a major triad in bars 3-4, 7-8 and 11-12 just to show you that you can do it. You play them as Dominant 7 and M6 chords also.

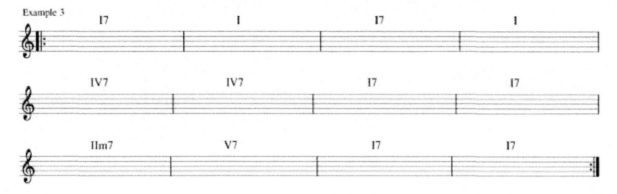

Example 3

As in the previous example, I wrote the "I" chord as either a triad or Dominant 7 chord. You could also play them all as M6 chords if you like or combine the Dominant 7, Major Triad and M6 qualities however you like.

The "main" variation here starts at bar 9. Instead of just a V7 chord, we have a IIm7 V7 progression as its replacement. The overall harmonic scheme doesn't change. This progression adds tension towards the I chord, so we consider those two bars as a "dominant section". It is a bit more interesting than playing V7 for two bars.

You could resolve it into a Major Triad or the I7 shown above. In either case you use the Dorian Mode for the IIm7 and the Mixolydian Mode for the V7.

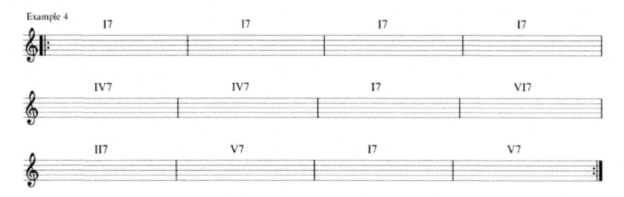

Example 4

In this example, we find an extended dominant sequence starting on bar eight and finally resolving into I7 in bar 11.

VI7 resolves into II7, which resolves into V7, which resolves into I7.

You could, technically speaking, play the I Blues or Minor Pentatonic Scale throughout the whole form and/or play Mixolydian Mode on each chord, BUT I really encourage you to use Mixolydian b6 (fifth mode of Melodic Minor) on the VI7 chord.

Our ears will be expecting to hear a IIm7 after that, but the effect of having a II7 instead sounds really nice. It gives the whole thing a bit more texture. A little "not very surprising" surprise.

By the way: You will encounter this and the next example at A LOT of jam sessions.

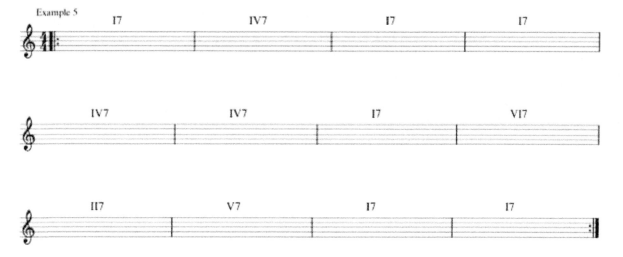

This is almost the same as the previous example. The only difference is the IV7 in the 2nd. bar. You should try playing the Lydian Dominant Mode over that one. It sounds really nice and jazzy. Your "Pentatonic-only" friends will notice.

Common Blues Progressions

Sergio Klein

Common Blues Progressions cont.

Sergio Klein

Example 5

| I7 | IV7 | I7 | I7 |

| IV7 | IV7 | I7 | VI7 |

| II7 | V7 | I7 | I7 |

Example 6

| I7 | I7 | I7 | I7 |

| IV7 | #IVdim | I7 | VI7 |

| IIm7 | V7 | I7 | I7 |

The "Parker Blues"

Charlie Parker, also known as "Bird" and "Yardbird", is one of the most famous and influential jazz musician of all times. There is certainly a "before" and "after" Parker.

He was a virtuoso saxophone player who was always stretching the boundaries of his instrument and music itself. He mastered harmony in such a way that it seemed to be instinctive to him. He matched his harmonic mastery with a brilliant melodic approach. For this, some say he is the Johan Sebastian Bach of Jazz.

Along with other musicians, such as the trumpet player Dizzy Gillespie (another genius) and drummer Max Roach, he is considered the founder of Bebop.

Bebop brought a whole new level of sophistication and complexity to jazz music. Its influence can be heard in almost any music style nowadays.

Not only did the harmony get more complex, but the rhythm and the tempos in which the music was being performed took everyone by surprise as well – and it's still fascinating to this day. Even now, Charlie Parker's music can be mind-blowing. It certainly blew mine... more than a couple of times.

Just listen to his solo on "Confirmation" and you will instantly know what I mean.

I'm serious! Go and do that right now!

As all good musicians do, he explored the possibilities the Blues had to offer, and as usually hardworking geniuses do, he came up with some really nice ideas.

This is what a "Parker Blues" looks like:

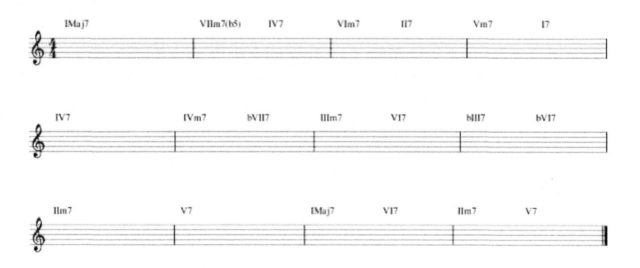

In the picture above, I wrote the Parker Blues the way it is supposed to be learned. Every chord is analyzed based on its relationship to the key in which we are playing, but the most important thing here is to know and understand which function each chord has to the next.
There is a lot going on here, so I'll write this in the key of C to make it easier to explain. In this chart, I analyzed each chord based on its relationship to the chords surrounding it, this way you can better see what Charlie Parker was doing.

Parker Blues in C:

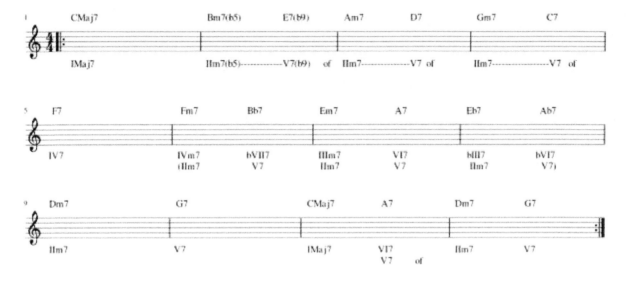

Let's analyze this step-by-step.

First measure:

In the first measure Charlie Parker used to play IMaj7 instead of I7, which would be the "typical" Blues way to play the I chord. Although sometimes he did indeed play it as a dominant 7 chord to get that "bluesy" sound while soloing, this is not what the rest of the band was playing.

Second measure:

Here is where he starts a series of II V's which will eventually resolve into the IV7 (F7) in bar five.

The Bm7(b5) and E7(b9) are no longer analyzed as VIIm7(b5) and VI7 respectively. Instead we analyze those two chords as a secondary IIm7(b5) V7(b9) of Am7.

Over the Bm7(b5) chord we play Locrian and over the A7(b9) you'll remember that we play 5th mode of Harmonic Minor: the Phrygian Dominant Mode.

Third measure:

Here we have another IIm7-V7. This one starts with Am7, the chord the previous IIm7 V7 resolved to. Am7 D7 resolves then to Gm7 at the beginning of the 3rd measure.

Don't use Aeolian mode on the VIm7 chord, as it is not functioning as a VIm7 of C.
Because the chord is now the IIm7 of G, we play the Dorian Mode.
Over D7 we play the Mixolydian Mode. As II7 in the key of C, it uses that mode as it is essentially a "Dorian Mode with a raised 3rd": 1   2   3   4   5   6   b7 = Mixolydian formula.

Fourth measure:

Here we have another IIm7-V7 which starts where the previous one resolves.
This time, it is the secondary IIm7-V7 of IV. And it resolves into IV7 in the fifth measure.

Over Gm7 we also play Dorian. Think of it as a "Mixolydian with a flatted 3rd".

Over C7 we also play Mixolydian, if related to the overall key of the tune, you can see it as a "Ionian with a flatted 7th".

Fifth measure:

This is where our "chain" of II-V's finally resolves to the IV7 chord, in this case, F7.
We call these II V patterns "sequential II V chains" or "extended II V chains". They are both different names for the same thing: a II V resolves into another one, and this resolves into another one and so on.

This tune is a Blues after all, so we need to resolve into the IV7 at the 5th measure to keep the form.

Sixth through eighth measures:

Here is where the real fun begins. I'll put those measures here again so it's easier to see what's going on. I'm no fan of scrolling up and down or going back and forth through pages. It's the way it is, so here you go:

Fm7	Bb7	Em7	A7	Eb7	Ab7
IVm7	bVII7	IIIm7	VI7	bIII7	bVI7
(IIm7	V7	IIm7	V7	IIm7	V7)

At first sight this looks like a series of II-V's descending chromatically, and it is, but its function is an extended dominant with a II before each V7. The key is that the "V" is actually the tritone substitution of the dominant chord on the next measure. You could write those three measures like this:

Bb7	A7	Ab7

Here I simply removed the II chord in each measure. Presented like this, you immediately realize what is really going on. Instead of using the V7 of each chord and then resolving it, Parker uses the tritone substitution of those implied V7 chords and then resolves them into another tritone substitution.
Bb7 is the tritone substitute of E7, resolves into A7.
A7 is the tritone substitution of Eb7, resolves into Ab7

This is the core idea, it works exactly as an extended dominant progression, but using tritone substitutions instead of the "normal" V7 chord.

He adds a IIm7 before each dominant 7 chord and *Voilà!* We get a "chromatic II V".

What I really like about how Charlie Parker did this in his tune "Blues for Alice" (exactly the blues we've been analyzing here), is how he continues it in measures 9 through 10:

9	Dm7	G7	CMaj7
	IIm7	V7	IMaj7

Remember: the last chord in measure eight is a Ab7 – the tritone substitution of G7.
I love what he did in these measures: he adds another II V to the chromatic II V chain, but this time he doubles the duration of each chord.

By doing this, he starts to generate more tension towards the upcoming IMaj7 chord. We begin to feel that THAT is the chord we were heading to the entire time. And the whole II V chain does indeed resolve into the IMaj7 chord in measure 11.

B-E-A-U-T-I-F-U-L

Yes, very beautiful indeed, but what do we play over that chromatic II V chain?

This progression is really hard to improvise over. Sure, you can play each II V in its own key centre and it will sound "correct". The real challenge, though, is to make it sound musical, not "predetermined" nor "mechanical".

Each II V from the chain is in a different key centre, but not only that, those key centres have almost no common notes to tie them together nicely… or so it seems.

Something you could do to start, is to use the third of the Dominant 7 chord at the end of each measure as a connecting note into the IIm7 at the beginning of the next measure. That 3rd from the V7 chord is also the minor 7th of the following IIm7 chord.

What I always recommend is to let the melody decide HOW you will play on every new key centre.

You can also use the repetition of a motive to connect chords. Just be careful of repeating it too often or in the same manner every time. Repetition is a powerful tool to make your ideas more recognizable, but done in the wrong way it can also produce monotony.

One thing you can do to practice this, is to choose a simple motive and develop it throughout the II V chain. Practice REALLY slow at first:

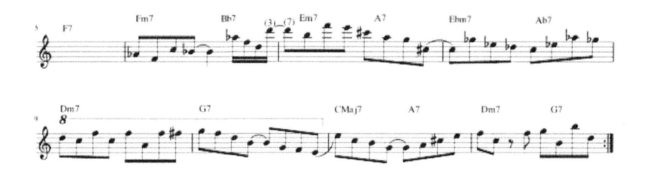

In this example I combined those two concepts, motive repetition/development and connecting the V7 and the following IIm7 at their common note.

Let's break it down:

-Motive:

Pretty simple. I'll call it "note goes down, from the second note jump up higher than the starting note and from there go down again".

It's a long name for a short idea, I know, but that's the way I think about motives. That way I feel free to change the intervals however I want without thinking about it too much. The important thing here is the "gesture" or "arc" the notes are forming. Also extremely VITAL: the rhythm.

Later when phrasing, to keep things coherent, I would change the intervals and keep the rhythm. If I change the rhythm, I would first subdivide one or more notes.

I did this on the Bb7 throughout the Em7 chord. Also notice that those two chords are connected at their shared note:

First, the unaltered motive is played over Fm7. On the second beat of Bb7 the motive appears again, but altered. The first eighth note of the motive is divided into two sixteenth-notes. The arc stays the same, but now two variations of the motive are tied together. The first is the one we play over Bb7 and it ties into the beginning of the motive over Em7. That D note is the point where both variations of the motive connect.

At that D note the variation of the motive consists of just changing the intervals. Besides that, the "longer note" is now at the beginning of the motive and not at the end of it, like in the original motive.

Over A7 we keep the rhythm of the original motive, but we change the intervals and direction of the melody. It starts the same: "note goes down", but then it keeps going down instead of jumping to a higher note.

You can think of that last note, the C#, as Db (b7 of Ebm7), as well. I used this note to connect A7 and Ebm7.

Here the development of the motive is quite obvious. The motive variation over Ebm7 is the same as over Fm7 in the previous measure. Over Ab7 I changed the motive a bit by changing the direction of the first two notes. The last two are still the same idea as in the original: "Higher note than the first two and then go down". In the next, measure we will use that "tail" of the motive to make a melodic connection.

As you can hear and see here, we are using that descending idea to make a coherent transition from one chord to the next. It is part of the first motive. By repeating it we actually transform this little idea into a second motive.

To avoid monotony, I changed the interval with each repetition. The F# note at the end of the measure is just a chromatic neighbor tone of the G note at the beginning of the next measure.

These two measures are really simple. We keep the rhythm of the original motive over G7, then we connect each motive as we connected them before: we extend the duration of the last note of the beat into the first note of the following beat. When changing direction over A7 our brain has no problem with it. The rhythm is the same so the motive stays coherent with the overall idea for these two measures.

This measure starts by playing motive 2 again. It makes "extra" sense too, because when we first used that motive as a motive in itself it was also over a Dm7 chord.

That F note just before the G7 chord starts is quite nice. It anticipates the repetition of motive 1 over that chord, strengthening the idea that "everything was about this motive the whole time".

We have deviated a bit from the original purpose of this book, which is to give you solid practice ideas to start getting the most common "harmonic situations" you will encounter as an improviser into your body, mind and ears.

I think we did a pretty good job of covering those concepts throughout the book until this point. Now you know harmony really well and can play the "correct" notes over any chord in any context.

Once those notes are in your fingers; once you hear them in your head and realize that you are indeed playing over chord changes with ease, then your body is telling you that you should start concentrating your efforts a bit more on your phrasing and on making your own melodies and learning how to get the most out of them.

This "Parker Blues" Unit was perfect to talk a bit about motives, repetition, etc. Those "extended II V chains" can be a trap sometimes and before you know it, your soloing over them can sound really predictable and boring. Almost like a "sticker" or a "parenthesis" in the middle of your solo.

Many fall into the trap of composing predetermined lines to play over those changes. This is a good idea when starting to play, but after a while it will really bother you. The best method is just to practice the concepts I gave you here (there are even more) really slow.

It may seem like you are progressing slower than you could be, but you will not be learning how to "save your butt" (that would be learning predetermined phrases to play over changes). You will be learning how to make MUSIC over those changes. That takes time indeed, but it will be a time 100% well invested.

Remember: "The dark side is not more powerful, just easier and seductive. In the end, consume you, it will".

In other words: "Do the real work now, so you don't get destroyed in a jam session later...

Epilogue

This is not the end of this book. These pages are just at the beginning of your musical journey. If you have been practicing what I've written for you here, you have come a long way already. I congratulate you for this. I know it can be frustrating sometimes, but I also know very well how fulfilling the reward feels, when you overcome the hardships of pushing yourself to really learn music and create your own artistic language.
The beauty of this book is that it focuses on all things you really should know, but at the same time it makes you get really involved in the process. It leaves every page open to your own ideas.

When the years go by, you will visit these pages less and less I hope, but when the time finally comes when you see yourself becoming this great artist you have always wanted to be - I'd like to think that, somehow you would have also learned to treasure the time you've spend working with this book, as I did working on it.

Be proud of your work, but don't become arrogant.
Don't be too hard on yourself, but don't become self-complaisant either.
Enjoy what you do and let it make you and others happy.

And as I said at the beginning of these pages:

Keep passing the torch!

Printed in Great Britain
by Amazon

54140214R00097